SUPPLY CHAIN MANAGEMENT

MRS. POORNIMA G | ASSISTANT PROFESSOR IN COMMERCE | A J K COLLEGE OF ARTS AND SCIENCE COIMBATORE

Made with ❤ on the Notion Press Platform
www.notionpress.com

Contents

Preface

This book is targeted toward an academic as well as a practitioner audience. On the academic side, it should be appropriate for B.Com and MBA students, engineering master's students, and senior undergraduate students interested in supply chain management and logistics. It should also serve as a suitable reference for both concepts as well as methodola ogy for practitioners in consulting and industry.

The book has grown from a course on supply chain management taught to second- year MBA students at the Kellogg School of Management at Northwestern University. The goal of this class was to cover not only high-level supply chain strategy and concepts but also to give students a solid understanding of the analytical tools necessary to solve supply chain problems. With this class goal in mind, our objective was to create a book that would develop an understanding of the following key areas and their interrelationships:

The strategic role of a supply chain
• The key strategic drivers of supply chain performance
• Analytic methodologies for supply chain analysis

Our first objective in this book is for the reader to learn the strategic importance of good supply chain design, planning, and operation for every firm. The reader will be able to understand how good supply chain management can be a competitive advantage, whereas weaknesses in the supply chain can hurt the performance of a firm. We use many examples to illustrate this idea and develop a framework for supply chain strategy. Within the strategic framework, we identify facilities, inventory, transportation, information, sourcing, and pricing as the key drivers of supply chain performance.

Our second goal in the book is to convey how these drivers may be used on a contceptual and practical level during supply chain design, planning, and operation to improve performance. We have included a case on Seven-Eleven Japan that can be used to illustrate how the company uses various drivers to improve supply chain performance. For each driver of supply chain performance, our goal is to provide readers with practical managerial levers and concepts that may be used to improve supply chain performance. Utilizing these managerial levers requires knowledge of analytic methodologies for supply chain analysis. Our third goal is to give the reader an understanding of these methodologies. Every methodological discussion is illustrated with its application in Excel. In this discussion, we also stress the managerial context in which they are used and the managerial levers for improvement that they support. The strategic frameworks and concepts discussed in the book are tied together through a variety of examples that show how a combination of concepts is needed to achieve significant increases in performance.

Acknowledgements

There are many people I would like to thank who helped us throughout this process. We thank the reviewer whose suggestions significantly improved the book, including Ms. K.Gowri, Assistant Professor, Bharathair University

We are grateful to the students at the AJK College of Arts and Science, Navakkarai, Coimbatore who suffered through typo-ridden drafts of earlier versions of the book. My Heartly thanks to Dr. Ajith Lal Finally, we would like to thank you, our readers, for reading and using this book. We hope it contributes to all of your efforts to improve the performance of companies and supply chains throughout the world. We would be pleased to hear your comments and suggestions for future editions of this text.

CHAPTER I

INTRODUCTION TO SUPPLY CHAIN MANAGEMENT

Supply Chain Management – Global Optimization – Importance – Key Issues – Inventory Management – Economic Lot Size model. Supply Contracts – Centralized vs. Decentralized System.

LEARNING OBJECTIVES:

After reading this chapter, you will be able to

- Discuss the goal of a supply chain and explain the impact of supply chain decisions on the success of a firm.
- Identify the three key supply chain decision phases and explain the significance of each one.
- Describe the cycle and push/pull views of a supply chain.
- Classify the supply chain macro processes in a firm.

In this chapter, we provide a conceptual understanding of what a supply chain is and the various issues that need to be considered when designing, planning, or operating a supply chain. We discuss the significance of supply chain decisions and supply chain performance for the success of a firm. We also provide several examples from different

1

industries to emphasize the variety of supply chain issues that companies need to consider at the strategic, planning, and operational levels.

INTRODUCTION

Supply chain management is the management of the flow of goods and services and includes all processes that transform raw materials into final products. It involves the active streamlining of a business's supply-side activities to maximize customer value and gain a competitive advantage in the marketplace. At the most fundamental level, supply chain management (SCM) is the management of the flow of goods, data, and finances related to a product or service, from the procurement of raw materials to the delivery of the product at its final destination. Examples of supply chain activities can include designing, farming, manufacturing, packaging, or transporting. A supply chain is the network of all the individuals, organizations, resources, activities, and technology involved in the creation and sale of a product. A supply chain encompasses everything from the delivery of source materials from the supplier to the manufacturer through to its eventual delivery to the end user.

Objectives

- Maximize the overall value generated the difference between what the final product is worth to the customer and the effort the supply chains expend in filling the request of the customer.

- Supply chain profitability is the difference between the revenue generated from the customer and the overall cost across the supply chain.
- It is the total profit to be shared across all supply chain stages.
- Supply chain success is measured in terms of supply chain profitability and not in terms of the profits at an individual stage.
- Revenue is from customers – positive cash flow.
- All other cash flows are simply fund exchanges that occur within the supply chain given that different stages have different owners.
- All flows of information, product, or funds generate costs within the supply chain.
- Supply chain management involves the management of flows between and among stages in a supply chain to maximize total supply chain profitability.

Supply chain management basically merges supply and demand management. It uses different strategies and approaches to view the entire chain and works efficiently at each and every step involved in the chain. Every unit that participates in the process must aim to minimize the costs and help the companies to improve their long-term performance, while also creating value for its stakeholders and customers. This process can also minimize the rates by eradicating unnecessary expenses, movements, and handling. Here we need to note that supply chain management and supply chain event management are two different topics to consider. The Supply Chain Event Management considers the factors that may interrupt the flow of an effective supply chain; possible scenarios are considered and accordingly, solutions are devised for them.

Important Benefits of Supply Chain Management

- Better collaboration with suppliers.
- Better quality control.
- Shipping optimization.
- Reduced inventory and overhead costs.
- Improved risk mitigation.
- Stronger cash flow.
- A more agile business.
- Better visibility and data analytics.

DECISION PHASES IN A SUPPLY CHAIN

Successful supply chain management requires many decisions relating to the flow of information, product, and funds. Each decision should be made to raise the supply chain surplus. These decisions fall into three categories or phases, depending on the frequency of each decision and the time frame during which a decision phase has an impact. As a result, each category of decisions must consider uncertainty over the decision horizon.

- **Supply Chain Strategy or Design:**

During this phase, a company decides how to structure the supply chain over the next several years. It decides what the chain's configuration will be, how resources will be allocated, and what processes each stage will perform. Strategic decisions made by companies include whether to outsource or perform a supply chain function in-house, the location and capacities of production and warehousing facilities, the products to be manufactured or stored at various locations, the modes of transportation to be made available along different shipping legs, and the type of information system to be utilized. PepsiCo Inc.'s decision in 2009 to purchase two of its largest bottlers is a supply chain design or strategic decision. A firm must ensure that the supply chain configuration supports its strategic objectives and increases the supply chain surplus during this phase. As the PepsiCo CEO announced in a news release on August 4, "while the existing model has served the system very well, the fully integrated beverage business will enable us to bring innovative products and packages to market faster, streamline our manufacturing and distribution systems and react more quickly to changes in the marketplace.

- **Supply Chain Planning:**

For decisions made during this phase, the time frame considered is a quarter to a year. Therefore, the supply chain's configuration determined in the strategic phase is fixed. This configuration establishes constraints within which planning must be done. The goal of planning is to maximize the supply chain surplus that can be generated over the planning horizon given the constraints established during the strategic or design phase. Companies start the planning phase with a forecast for the coming year (or a comparable time frame) of demand and other factors such as costs and prices in different markets. Planning includes making decisions regarding which markets will be supplied from which locations, the subcontracting of manufacturing, the inventory policies to be followed, and the timing and size of marketing and price promotions. For example, steel giant ArcelorMittal's decisions regarding markets supplied by a production facility and target production quantities at each location are classified as planning decisions. Planning establishes parameters within which a supply chain will function over a specified period of time.

- **Supply Chain Operation:**

The time horizon here is weekly or daily. During this phase, companies make decisions regarding individual customer orders. At the operational level, supply chain configuration is considered fixed, and planning policies are already defined. The goal of supply chain operations is to handle incoming customer orders in the best possible manner. During this phase, firms allocate inventory or production to individual orders, set a date that an order is to be filled, generate pick lists at a warehouse, allocate an order to a particular shipping mode and shipment, set delivery schedules of trucks, and place replenishment orders. Because operational decisions are being made in the short term (minutes, hours, or days), there is less uncertainty about demand information. Given the constraints established by the configuration and planning policies, the goal during the operation phase is to exploit the reduction of uncertainty and optimize performance.

The Advantages of Supply Chain Management System:
Businesses have many advantages of supply chain management systems. One of the competitive advantages is that it allows you to decrease the inherent risks when you're buying raw materials and selling products or services. An effective supply chain can help companies to meet the demand for their products and meet customer

expectations. It can also improve the quality of products and cut down on waste. By using a supply chain management system, a company can effectively monitor its entire supply chain and identify issues early on, which can save time and money in the long run. There are many benefits of supply chain management, such as efficient rates, decrease cost, increased outputs, and increased profit levels, and they are discussed here in detail.

Goals of Supply Chain Management

- Every firm strives to match supply with demand in a timely fashion with the most efficient use of resources. Here are some of the important goals of supply chain management:
- Supply chain partners work collaboratively at different levels to maximize resource productivity, construct standardized processes, remove duplicate efforts and minimize inventory levels.
- Minimization of supply chain expenses is very essential, especially when there are economic uncertainties in companies regarding their wish to conserve capital.
- Cost efficient and cheap products are necessary, but supply chain managers need to concentrate on value creation for their customers.
- Exceeding the customers' expectations on a regular basis is the best way to satisfy them.
  Increased expectations of clients for higher product variety, customized goods, off-season availability of inventory and rapid fulfillment at a cost comparable to in-store offerings should be matched.

To meet consumer expectations, merchants need to leverage inventory as a shared resource and utilize the distributed order management technology to complete orders from the optimal node in the supply chain.

Lastly, supply chain management aims at contributing to the financial success of an enterprise. In addition to all the points highlighted above, it aims at leading enterprises using the supply chain to improve differentiation, increase sales, and penetrate new markets. The objective is to drive competitive benefit and shareholder value. Supply chain management is a process used by companies to ensure that their supply chain is efficient and cost-effective. A supply chain is the collection of steps that a company takes to transform raw materials into a final product. *The five basic components of supply chain management are discussed below:*

Plan:

The initial stage of the supply chain process is the planning stage. We need to develop a plan or strategy in order to address how the products and services will satisfy the demands and necessities of the customers. In this stage, the planning should mainly focus on designing a strategy that yields maximum profit. For managing all the resources required for designing products and providing services, a strategy has to be designed by the companies. Supply chain management mainly focuses on planning and developing a set of metrics.

Develop (Source):

After planning, the next step involves developing or sourcing. In this stage, we mainly concentrate on building a strong relationship with suppliers of the raw materials required for production. This involves not only identifying dependable suppliers but also determining different planning methods for shipping, delivery, and payment of the product. Companies need to select suppliers to deliver the items and services they require to develop their product. So in this stage, the supply chain managers need to construct a set of pricing, delivery and payment processes with suppliers and also create the metrics for controlling and improving the relationships. Finally, the supply chain managers can combine all these processes for handling their goods and services inventory. This handling comprises receiving and examining shipments, transferring them to the manufacturing facilities and authorizing supplier payments.

Make:

The third step in the supply chain management process is the manufacturing or making of products that were demanded by the customer. In this stage, the products are designed, produced, tested, packaged, and synchronized for delivery. Here, the task of the supply chain manager is to schedule all the activities required for manufacturing, testing, packaging and preparation for delivery. This stage is considered as the most metric-intensive unit of the supply chain, where firms can gauge the quality levels, production output and worker productivity.

Delivery:

The fourth stage is the delivery stage. Here the products are delivered to the customer at the destined location by the supplier. This stage is basically the logistics phase, where customer orders are accepted and delivery of the goods is planned. The delivery stage is often referred to as logistics, where firms collaborate for the receipt of orders from customers, establish a network of warehouses, pick carriers to deliver products to customers, and set up an invoicing system to receive payments.

Return :

The last and final stage of supply chain management is referred to as the return. In this stage, defective or damaged goods are returned to the supplier by the customer. Here, the companies need to deal with customer queries and respond to their complaints, etc. This stage often tends to be a problematic section of the supply chain for many companies. The planners of the supply chain need to discover a responsive and flexible network for accepting damaged, defective and extra products back from their customers and facilitating the return process for customers who have issues with delivered products. Supply chain management can be defined as a systematic flow of materials, goods, and related information among suppliers, companies, retailers, and consumers.

TYPES

There are three different types of flow in supply chain management:

- Material flow
- Information/Data flow
- Money flow

Let us consider each of these flows in detail and also see how effectively they are applicable to Indian companies.

Material Flow:

Material flow includes a smooth flow of an item from the producer to the consumer. This is possible through various warehouses among distributors, dealers, and retailers. The main challenge we face is in ensuring that the material flows as inventory quickly without any stoppage through different points in the chain. The quicker it moves, the better it is for the enterprise, as it minimizes the cash cycle. The item can also flow from the consumer to the producer for any kind of repairs, or exchange for an end-of-life material. Finally, completed goods flow from customers to their consumers through different agencies. A process known as 3PL is in place in this scenario. There is also an internal flow within the customer company.

Information Flow:

Information/data flow comprises the request for quotation, purchase orders, monthly schedules, engineering change requests, quality complaints, and reports on supplier performance from the customer side to the supplier. From the producer's side to the consumer's side, the information flow consists of the presentation of the company, offering confirmation of purchase order, reports on action taken on deviation, dispatch details; report on inventory, invoices, etc. For a successful supply chain, regular interaction is necessary between the producer and the consumer. In many instances, we can see that other partners like distributors, dealers, retailers, and logistic service providers participate in the information network. In addition to this, several departments on the producer and consumer side are also a part of the information loop. Here we need to note that the internal information flow with the customer for in-house manufacture is different.

Money Flow:

On the basis of the invoice raised by the producer, the clients examine the order for correctness. If the claims are correct, money flows from the clients to the respective producer. The flow of money is also observed from the producer side to the clients in the form of debit notes. In short, to achieve an efficient and effective supply chain, it is essential to manage all three flows properly with minimal effort. It is a difficult task for a supply chain manager to identify which information is critical for decision-making. Therefore, he or she would prefer to have the visibility of all flows at the click of a button. After understanding the basic flows involved in supply chain management, we need to consider the different elements present in this flow. Thus, the different components of the flow of the supply chain are described below.

TRANSPORTATION

Transportation or shipment is necessary for an uninterrupted and seamless supply. The factors that have an impact on a shipment are economic uncertainty and instability, varying fuel prices, customers' expectations, globalization, improvised technologies, changing transportation industry, and labor laws. The major elements that influence transportation should be considered, as it is completely dependent on these factors for order completion as well as for ensuring that all the flows work properly. *The major factors are:*

Long-term Decisions

Transportation managers should acknowledge the supply freight flow and accordingly design the network layout. Now, when we say the long-term decision, we mean that the transportation manager has to select what should be the primary mode of transportation. The manager has to understand the product flows, volume, frequency, seasonality, physical features of products, and special handling necessities, if any. In addition to this, the manager has to make decisions as to the extent of outsourcing to be done for each and every product. While considering all these factors, he should carefully consider the fact that the networks need not be constant.

For example, in order to transport stock to regional cross-dock facilities for sorting, packaging, and brokering small loads to individual customers, stock destinations can be assembled through contract transportation providers.

Lane Operation Decisions:

These functional decisions stress daily freight operations. Here, the transportation managers work on real-time information on products' requirements at different system nodes and must collaborate on every move of the product that is both inbound and outbound shipping lanes so as to satisfy the demands of their service at the minimal possible cost. Managers who make good decisions easily handle information and utilize the opportunities for their own profit and assure that the product is moved to them immediately, whenever it is demanded, that too in the right quantity. At the same time, they are saving costs on transportation also.

For example, a shipment has landed from a supplier who is based in New Jersey, and in the same week, a product needs to be dispatched to New York as it becomes available for movement. If the manager is aware of this information in advance, he would prepare everything as per the demand and the products could be shipped out immediately.

Choice and Mode of Carrier:

A very important decision to be made is to choose the mode of transportation. With the improvement in the means of transportation, modes of transport that were not available in the traditional transportation modes in the past can now be a preferred choice.

For example, rail container service may offer a package that is cost-efficient and effective as compared to motor transport. While making a decision, the manager has to consider the service criteria that need to be met, like the delivery time, date special handling requirements, while also taking into consideration the element of cost, which would be an important factor.

Dock Level Operations:

This involves the last level of decision-making. This comprises planning, routing, and scheduling. **For example,** if a carriage is being loaded with different customers' orders, the function of the dock-level managers is to assure that the driver is informed of the most efficient route and that loads are placed in the order of the planned stops.

Warehousing:

Warehousing plays a vital role in the supply chain process. In today's industry, the demands and expectations of customers are undergoing tremendous change. We want everything at our doorstep – that too at an efficient price. We can say that the management of warehousing functions demands a distinct merging of engineering, IT, human resources, and supply chain skills. To neutralize the efficiency of inbound functions, it is ideal to accept materials in an immediately storable conveyance, like a pallet, case, or box. Labeling the structure, tool selection, and business process demand the types and quantities of orders that are processed. Further, the number of stock-keeping units (SKUs) in the distribution Centre is a crucial consideration. The Warehouse Management System (WMS) leads the products to their storage location where they should be stored. The required functionality for the completion and optimization of receiving, storing, and shipping functions are then supplied.

Sourcing and Procurement:

Sourcing and procurement are vital parts of supply chain management. The company decides if it wants to perform all the exercises internally or if it desires to get them done by any other independent firm. This is commonly referred to as the make vs. buy decision, which we will be discussing in brief in another chapter.

RETURNS MANAGEMENT

Returns management can be defined as the management that invites the merger of challenges and opportunities for inbound logistics. A cost-effective reverse logistics program links the available supply of returns with the product information and demand for repairable items or re-captured materials. We have three pillars that support returns management processes. *These are as follows:*

Speed: It is a must to have quick and easy returns management and automate decisions regarding whether to produce return material authorizations (RMAs) and if so, how to process them. Basically, the tools of speed return processing include automated workflows, labels & attachments, and user profiles.

Visibility: For improving visibility and predictability, information needs to be captured initially in the process, ideally prior to delivering the return to the receiving dock. The most effective and easily implementable approaches for obtaining visibility are web-based portals, carrier integration, and bar-coded identifiers.

Control: In the case of returns management, synchronizing material movements is a common issue that needs to be handled. The producers need to be very cautious and pay close attention to receipts and reconciliation and update the stakeholders on impending quality issues. In this case, reconciliation activates visibility and control all over the enterprise. The key control points in this process are regulatory compliance, reconciliation, final disposition, and quality assurance.

Software solutions can assist in speeding up returns management by supporting user profiles and workflows that state supply chain partners and processes, by labeling and documentation that tracks the material along with the web-based portals, and by exception-based reporting to deliver information for timely reconciliation. These characteristics, when executed with the three pillars mentioned above, support a reliable and predictable returns process to count value across the company.

Post-Sales Service : Now that the ordered shipment is over, what is the next step? The post-sales service in the supply chain tends to be an increasingly essential factor as businesses offer solutions instead of products. The post-sales services comprise selling spare parts, installing upgrades, performing inspections, maintenance and repairs, offering training & education, and consulting. Presently, with the growing demands of the clients, a high volume of after-sales service proves to be a profitable business. Here, the services are basically heterogeneous and the value-added services are different from those provided prior to sales service.

Decision Phases: Decision phases can be defined as the different stages involved in supply chain management for taking an action or decision related to some product or service. Successful supply chain management requires decisions on the flow of information, product, and funds that fall into three decision phases. Here we will be discussing the three main decision phases involved in the entire process of the supply chain. The three phases are described below:

SUPPLY CHAIN STRATEGY

In this phase, decisions are taken by the management mostly. The decision to be made considers the sections like long-term prediction and involves the price of goods that are very expensive if it goes wrong. It is very important to study the market conditions at this stage. These decisions consider the prevailing and future conditions of the market. They comprise the structural layout of the supply chain. After the layout is prepared, the tasks and duties of each are laid out. All the strategic decisions are taken by the higher authority or senior management. These decisions include deciding on manufacturing the material, factory location, which should be easy for transporters to load material and to dispatch at their mentioned location, location of warehouses for storage of completed products or goods, and many more.

Supply Chain Planning:

Supply chain planning should be done according to the demand and supply view. In order to understand customers' demands, market research should be done. The second thing to consider is awareness and updated information about the competitors and strategies used by them to satisfy their customer's demands and requirements. As we know, different markets have different demands and should be dealt with with a different approach. This phase includes it all, starting from predicting the market demand to which market will be provided the finished goods to which plant is planned in this stage. All the participants or employees involved with the company should make efforts to make the entire process as flexible as they can. A supply chain design phase is considered successful if it performs well in short-term planning.

Supply Chain Operations:

The third and last decision phase consists of the various functional decisions that are to be made instantly within minutes, hours, or days. The objective behind this decisional phase is minimizing uncertainty and performance optimization. Starting from handling the customer order to supplying the customer with that product, everything is included in this phase. **For example,** imagine a customer demanding an item manufactured by your company. Initially, the marketing department is responsible for taking the order and forwarding it to the production department and inventory department. The production department then responds to the customer demand by sending the demanded item to the warehouse through a proper medium and the distributor sends it to the customer within a time frame. All the departments engaged in this process need to work with an aim of improving performance and minimizing uncertainty. Supply chain performance measures can be defined as an approach to judging the performance of a supply chain system. Supply chain performance measures can broadly be classified into two categories:

Qualitative Measures: For example, customer satisfaction and product quality.

Quantitative Measures: For example, order-to-delivery lead time, supply chain response time, flexibility, resource utilization, and delivery performance.

Here, we will be considering the quantitative performance measures only. The performance of a supply chain can be improvised by using a multi-dimensional

Important Benefits of Supply Chain

Higher Efficiency Rate:

When your business is able to incorporate supply chains, integrated logistics, and product innovation strategies, you'll be in a great position to not only predict demand as well as to act accordingly. And this is, without any doubt, one of the main benefits of supply chain management. Why? When your business implements supply chain management systems, it will be able to adjust more dynamically to fluctuating economies, emerging markets, and shorter product life cycles.

Decrease Cost Effects:

One of the advantages of supply chain management is the costs decrease in different areas. The most important ones are:

- Improves your inventory system;
- Adjusts the storage space for finished goods which eliminates damage to resources;
- Improves your system's responsiveness to the actual customer's requirements;
- Improves your relationship with both distributors and vendors.

Increases Output:

Communication improvement is among the main advantages of supply chain management. This adds up to the coordination and collaboration with shipping and transport companies, vendors, and suppliers.

Increases Your Business Profit Level:

When you place your business open to new technologies and improved collaboration within the different areas, you can be sure that this will ultimately increase your business profit level.

Boost Cooperation Level:

When we're talking about the most successful businesses right now, one of the things they all have in common is communication. In fact, when there is a lack of communication, your vendors and distributors have no idea about what's going on. So, this is definitely one of the main advantages of supply chain management. Plus, when you also open your doors and embrace technology, you can also take advantage of the fact that people don't even need to share the same space in order to be true communication. Communication among the different areas of your business will allow you to have faster access to forecasts, reporting, quotations, and statuses, among many other plans in real-time.

No More Delays in Processes:

The benefits of supply chain management include the fact that through communication, you can actually lower any delays in processes. Since everyone is aware of what they're doing as well as what others are doing, this will mitigate any late shipments from vendors, logistical errors in distribution channels, and hold-ups on production lines.

Enhanced Supply Chain Network:

It's not easy to maintain a sustainable supply chain management system. According to some of its advocates, one of the best ways to do it is by using a combination of lean practices (like waste removal, for example) with agile. The supply chain strategic planning and combining all the information gathered on the different sectors of your business will allow you to have an enhanced supply chain network.

MRS. POORNIMA G, ASSISTANT PROFESSOR IN COMMERCE, A J K
COLLEGE OF ARTS AND SCIENCE COIMBATORE

GLOBAL OPTIMIZATION IN SUPPLY CHAIN MANAGEMENT

Global optimization is a branch of applied mathematics and numerical analysis that attempts to find the global minima or maxima of a function or a set of functions on a given set. Global optimization or global search refers to searching for the global optima. A global optimization algorithm, also called a global search algorithm, is intended to locate a global optimum. It is suited to traversing the entire input search space and getting close to (or finding exactly) the extreme of the function.

Supply Chain Optimization Definition

Supply chain optimization refers to the tools and processes by which manufacturing and distribution supply chain performance and efficiency are improved, taking into account all constraints. Supply chain network optimization technologies use sophisticated algorithms and analytics to balance supply and demand in such a manner that sufficient raw materials are procured for manufacturing and distribution to meet customer expectations at the highest cost efficiency.

Optimize a Supply Chain Network

Logistics and supply chain optimization is achieved with the use of sophisticated analytics and statistical software, which uses historical customer demand data in order to predict future inventory demand with the highest rate of accuracy. Supply chain inventory optimization results in an inventory level that is known as "model stock." The forecast demand is used to develop a supply-chain manufacturing and distribution management strategy, which typically includes the following phases:

- Supply chain design optimization: focuses on warehouse locations, product flows within the warehouse facilities network, manufacturing schedules, and demand planning
- Supply chain planning optimization: determines how to manufacture and distribute products and/or services in a way that will balance supply and demand, and meet the forecast demand at the highest profitability
- Supply chain execution optimization: focuses on global trade management, inventory management, order management systems, real-time decision support, supply chain visibility, and transportation management

Supply chain optimization software solutions are capable of forecasting, balancing supply and demand, organizing and managing inventory and deliveries, and managing supply chain design, supply chain planning systems, and execution on a granular level. Inventory and supply chain optimization solutions are integrated into replenishment systems distribution requirements planning in order to seamlessly and precisely maintain the model stock profile in real time.

Supply chain network optimization tools include sophisticated optimization algorithms, which are capable of accounting for load and unloading rules, load stability regarding decreasing transportation costs, palletizing logic, stack ability constraints, and warehouse efficiency. Standard Deviation and Mean Absolute Deviation techniques may be applied to determine the amount of additional stock that should be maintained in inventory to mitigate risk of material shortfalls caused by unpredictable demand.

Modern supply chain optimization technologies typically provide a platform on which supply chain managers and supply chain optimization analysts gain real-time end-to-end visibility of supply chain operations; standardize, synchronize, and automate business processes and execution; and leverage machine learning capabilities and AI for supply chain optimization.

Benefits of Supply Chain Optimization

Advantages of supply chain network architecture optimization may include:

- Reduced surplus inventory
- Lower logistics cost levels
- Improved customer service due to better forecasting and improved availability
- Reduced time to act on supply chain issues and respond to market disruptions
- Simplified supplier on boarding and collaboration
- Decreased lead times
- Reduced time, total cost, and risk associated with qualifying and managing new suppliers
- Better resiliency, agility, and predictability in mitigating risks and maintaining business continuity.

Supply chain Performance, Strategic Fit, and Competitive Advantage-text:

Business environment and business operations do not function in isolation. Michael. E. Porter advocates that the competitive advantage of a nation depends on how Upgraded and innovative the firms in an industry. Firms today have realized that products of two firms might not be differentiated but the processes that are unique for each firm defines customer value creation. This has led to the strategic outlook of the supply chain.

This module on supply chain management with three lessons focuses on

- Business Environment and Supply Chain Competitiveness.
- Strategic Supply Chain Management - Customer Value Creation, Performance and Fit
- Drivers and Challenges of Supply Chain.

BUSINESS ENVIRONMENT AND SUPPLY CHAIN COMPETITIVENESS

The business environment consists of forces and factors that are beyond the control of the business but influences management decisions. This indicates that a conducive business environment defines industry existence and a firm's adaptation to domestic demand and business environment shapes its competitiveness through innovation and up-gradation. The forces in the business environment that impact the competitiveness of industry are Regulatory, Economic, Social, and Technological commonly known as REST might because the rest of the business decisions depend on these factors.

MRS. POORNIMA G, ASSISTANT PROFESSOR IN COMMERCE, A J K
COLLEGE OF ARTS AND SCIENCE COIMBATORE

The Regulatory business environment is formulated by the government legislations, Industrial Policies, EXIM policies, tariff and non-traffic barriers, regulations, and controls (resource, price, and market controls), and non-regulatory measures for sustainable industrial growth, infrastructure development, citizen well-being, and job creation. The Economic environment indicates the resource availability and allocation, demographic dividend, purchase power and consumption, savings and expenditure, In simple words, each operation or activity of a firm should be designed and implemented to leverage the opportunities and threats of the business environment, and supply chain management is not an exemption. The business environment and the related supply chain decisions are discussed based on some illustrative factors that impact the construction industry specifically the housing sector in India.

Some of the regulatory environments that have a high impact on the housing sector are:

1. Economic housing for all is the thrust area of government,
2. High taxation for buying and selling a house,
3. Transparency in registration and approval for construction and facilities,
4. Regulations and controls on resources like cement, s,and and iron and steel for environmental sustainability
5. Linkage of citizen cards and PAN cards for all transactional processes.

The Economic Environment Indicates that

- Disposable incomes have accelerated habits of consumption,
- Spiraling prices and inflation has increased the cost of housing.
- Interest rates on loan and tax concessions encourage investment in the housing sector.

The impact of environmental economics on replenishing natural resources, renewable energy, and carbon footprints indicates the need for resource substitutes and processes that are sustainable.

The Social Environment that Impacts Today's Housing Sectors are

1. Existence of nuclear families and demand for small houses,
2. High mobility and nuclear families have led to a lack of social networks and demand for community housing with proximity to all facilities with safety.
3. Changing consumption patterns indicate a house as a luxury with unique interiors, home furniture, and appliances.

The environmental and health consciousness of the customers creates demand for facilities like walking space and gym, kitchen gardens, renewable energy sources, and so on within the housing community.

Supply Chains do to Cope with these Situations:

Supply chains should leverage on supply-side commoditization (that is the purchase of standardized raw materials and facilities) and demand-side customization (End product designs and delivery are unique for each customer)

1. Supply chain management is about monitoring the business environments and foreseeing the changes to ensure a demand-driven supply chain supported by strategic sourcing and supplier alliances.
2. Changes in legislation and non -regulatory supports affect the availability and cost of supplies, and lead time. Responsive supply chains to identify transactional and collaborative relationships with government bodies and associations lead to competitive advantage.
3. Supply chain management processes can be standardized and digitalized to suit the regulatory processes.
4. Supply chains today are not only about interacting with raw material and component suppliers but also networking for outsourcing facilities and processes.
5. Environmental consciousness and social responsibilities should be inbuilt at all points of the supply chain through lean and green supply chain practices.

Important of Supply Chain Management

Modern supplies chains help improve living standards by enabling consumers to buy essential products at lower costs. This is because an effective supply chain streamlines the process of getting products to market, and ultimately to consumers.

Some key reasons why supply chain management is important to include:

Basic Life Necessities : Through supply chain management, individuals access necessities such as food and clothing, as well as life-saving medicines and health care products.

Power and Light: People use electrical energy for homes and businesses for light, heat, and air conditioning. The energy supply chain involves the transformation of raw materials into usable energy and uses supply chain management principles to bring energy resources to consumers.

Infrastructure : Interstate highway systems, railroads, ports, and airports facilitate the exchange of goods between businesses and consumers.

Jobs: Supply chain management plays a critical role in job creation. Supply chain professionals work in areas such as transportation, warehousing, inventory management, packaging and logistics information.

TYPES OF OPTIMIZATION TECHNIQUE:

Major Issues Facing Supply Chain Managers

- Managing customer expectations. One of the challenges of effective supply chain management is managing customer expectations. ...
- Managing suppliers. ...
- Maintaining quality and sustainability. ...
- Access to data. ...
- Risk mitigation

Three Key Issues in Supply Chain Management

Key Issue 1: Globalization. *Globalization presents several critical supply chain management challenges to enterprises and organizations.*

Key Issue 2 : Fast-changing Markets.

Key Issue 3 : Quality and Compliance.

SCM- PERFORMANCE MEASURES

Strategy, which addresses how the company needs to provide services to diverse customer demands.

Quantitative Measures:

Mostly the measures taken for measuring the performance may be somewhat similar to each other, but the objective behind each segment is very different from the other. A quantitative measure is the assessment used to measure the performance and compare or track the performance or products. We can further divide the quantitative measures of supply chain performance into two types. They are:

- Non-financial measures
- Financial measures

Non-Financial Measures

The metrics of **non-financial measures** comprise cycle time, customer service level, inventory levels, resource utilization ability to perform, flexibility, and quality. In this section, we will discuss the first four dimensions of the metrics:

<u>Cycle Time:</u>

Cycle time is often called the lead time. It can be simply defined as the end-to-end delay in a business process. For supply chains, cycle time can be defined as the business processes of interest, supply chain process and the order-to-delivery process. In the cycle time, we should learn about two types of lead times. *They are as follows:*

1. Supply chain lead time
2. Order-to-delivery lead time

The order-to-delivery lead time can be defined as the time of delay in the middle of the placement of order by a customer and the delivery of products to the customer. In case the item is in stock, it would be similar to the distribution lead time and order management time. If the ordered item needs to be produced, it would be the summation of supplier lead time, manufacturing lead time, distribution lead time and order management time. The supply chain process lead time can be defined as the time taken by the supply chain to transform the raw materials into final products along with the time required to reach the products to the customer's destination address.

Hence it comprises supplier lead time, manufacturing lead time, distribution lead time and the logistics lead time for transport of raw materials from suppliers to plants and for shipment of semi-finished/finished products in and out of intermediate storage points. Lead time in supply chains is governed by the halts in the interface because of the interfaces between suppliers and manufacturing plants, between plants and warehouses, between distributors and retailers and many more. Lead time compression is a crucial topic to discuss due to the time based competition and the collaboration of lead time with inventory levels, costs, and customer service levels.

<u>Customer Service Level</u>:

The customer service level in a supply chain is marked as an operation of multiple unique performance indices. Here we have three measures to gauge performance. They are as follows:

Order Fill Rate: The order fill rate is the portion of customer demands that can be easily satisfied from the stock available. For this portion of customer demands, there is no need to consider the supplier lead time and the manufacturing lead time. The order fill rate could be with respect to a central warehouse or a field warehouse or stock at any level in the system.

Stock Out Rate: It is the reverse of order fill rate and marks the portion of orders lost because of a stock out.

Backorder Level: This is yet another measure, which is the gauge of a total number of orders waiting to be filled.

Probability of on-Time Delivery: It is the portion of customer orders that are completed on-time, i.e., within the agreed-upon due date.

In order to maximize the customer service level, it is important to maximize order fill rate, minimize stock out rate, and minimize backorder levels.

<u>Inventory Levels</u>:

As the inventory-carrying costs increase the total costs significantly, it is essential to carry sufficient inventory to meet the customer demands. In a supply chain system, inventories can be further divided into four categories.

1. Raw materials
2. Work-in-process, i.e., unfinished and semi-finished sections
3. Finished goods inventory
4. Spare parts

Every inventory is held for a different reason. It's a must to maintain optimal levels of each type of inventory. Hence gauging the actual inventory levels will supply a better scenario of system efficiency.

Resource Utilization:

In a supply chain network, huge variety of resources is used. These different types of resources available for different applications are mentioned below.

Manufacturing resources: Include the machines, material handlers, tools, etc.

- **Storage resources**: Comprise warehouses, automated storage and retrieval systems.
- **Logistics resources**: Engage trucks, rail transport, air-cargo carriers, etc.
- **Human resources**: Consist of labor, scientific and technical personnel
- **Financial resources**: Include working capital, stocks, etc.

In the resource utilization paradigm, the main motto is to utilize all the assets or resources efficiently in order to maximize customer service levels, reduce lead times and optimize inventory levels.

SCM- STRATEGIC SOURCING

Financial Measures:

The measures taken for gauging different fixed and operational costs related to a supply chain are considered the financial measures. Finally, the key objective to be achieved is to maximize the revenue by maintaining low supply chain costs. There is a hike in prices because of the inventories, transportation, facilities, operations, technology, materials, and labour. Generally, the financial performance of a supply chain is assessed by considering the following items:

- Cost of raw materials.
- Revenue from goods sold.
- Activity-based costs like the material handling, manufacturing, assembling rates etc.
- Inventory holding costs
- Transportation costs
- Cost of expired perishable goods
- Penalties for incorrectly filled or late orders delivered to customers
- Credits for incorrectly filled or late deliveries from suppliers
- Cost of goods returned by customers
- Credits for goods returned to suppliers

In short, we can say that the financial performance indices can be merged as one by using key modules such as activity based costing, inventory costing, transportation costing, and inter- company financial transactions.

Strategic Sourcing can be defined as a collective and organized approach to supply chain management that defines the way information is gathered and used so that an organization can leverage its consolidated purchasing power to find the best possible values in the marketplace. We cannot build up the significance of operating in a collaborative manner. Several decades have witnessed a major transformation in the profession of supply chain, from the purchasing agent comprehension, where staying in repository was the criterion, to emerging into a supply chain management surrounding, where working with cross-functional and cross location teams is important, to achieve success.

Strategic sourcing is organized because of the necessity of some methodology or process. It is collective because one of the most essential necessities for any successful strategic sourcing attempt is of receiving operational components, apart from the procurement, engaged in the decision-making and assessment process. The process of strategic processing is a step-by-step approach. There are seven distinct steps engaged in the process of strategic processing. These steps are explained below in brief.

Understanding the Spend Category

The first three steps involved in strategic sourcing are carried out by the sourcing team. In this first stage, the team needs to do a complete survey on the total expenditure. The team ensures that it acknowledges every aspect of the spending category itself.

The five major regions that are analyzed in the first stage are as follows:

Complete previous expenditure records and volumes.
Expenditures are divided by items and sub-items.
Expenditures by division, department, or user.
Expenditures by the supplier.
Future demand projections or budgets.

For example, if the classification is grooved packaging at a customer goods company, the team has to acknowledge the description of the classification, application patterns and the reason behind specification of particular types and grades specified. Stakeholders at all functioning units and physical locations are to be determined. Logistics, for instance, needs an updated report regarding the transportation specifications and marketing requirements to acknowledge some quality or environmentally applicable features.

Supplier Market Assessment:

The second step includes frequent assessment of the supplier market for pursuing substitute suppliers to present incumbents. A thorough study of the supplier marketplace dynamics and current trends is done. The major element of the key products design is should- cost. Along with it, an analysis on the major suppliers' sub-tier marketplace and examination for any risks or new opportunities are also important.

Now, it is not recommended to analyse the should-cost for every item. There are many instances where conservative strategic sourcing techniques tend to work better. But in the instances where the application of strategic sourcing is not applicable, the should cost analysis supplies a valuable tool that drives minimizing of cost and regular progress efforts of the supplier.

Supplier Survey:

The third step is developing a supplier analysis for both incumbent and potential substitute suppliers. This analysis assists in examining the skills and abilities of a supplier. In the meanwhile, data collected from incumbent suppliers is used for verifying spend information that suppliers have from their sales systems.

The survey team considers the above-mentioned areas for gathering information. The areas are as follows:

1. Feasibility
2. Capability
3. Maturity
4. Capacity

The analysis is done to examine the potential and skills of the market to satisfy the customer demands. This analysis helps in the examination done at the initial stage to find out if the proposed project is feasible and can be delivered by the identified supply base. This analysis also supplies an initial caution of the customer demands to the market and enables suppliers to think about how they would react to and fulfill demand. Here the motto is to motivate the appropriate suppliers with the right structural layout to respond to the demands.

Building the Strategy:

The fourth step comprises constructing the sourcing strategy. The merger of the first three steps supports the necessary elements for the sourcing strategy. For every region or category, the strategy depends on answering the questions given below.

- How willing is the marketplace to oppose the supplier?
- How supportive are the clients of a firm for testing incumbent supplier relationships?
- What are the substitutes for the competitive assessment?

Generally, these substitutes opt for when a purchasing firm has little leverage over its supply base. They will depend on the belief that the suppliers will share the profits of a new strategy. Thus, we say that the sourcing strategy is an accumulation of all the drivers thus far mentioned.

RFx REQUEST

Mostly, the competitive approach is applied in general cases. In this approach, a request for proposal or bid needs to be prepared (e.g., RFP, RFQ, e RFQ, ITT) for most spend classifications or groups. This defines and clarifies all the needs of all prequalified suppliers. The request should comprise product or service specifications, delivery and service requirements, assessment criteria, pricing structure, and financial terms and conditions. In the fifth stage, an interaction plan needs to be executed to allure maximum supplier interest. It must be ensured that each and every supplier is aware that they are competing on a level playing field. After sending the RFP to all suppliers, it is to be confirmed that they are given enough time to respond. In order to motivate a greater response, follow-up messages should also be sent.

Selection:

This step is all about selecting and negotiating with suppliers. The sourcing team is advised to apply its assessment constraints to the responses generated by the suppliers. If information across the limitation of RFP response is required, it can be simply asked for. If done correctly, the settlement process is conducted first with a larger set of suppliers and then shortlisted to a few finalists. If the sourcing team utilizes an electronic negotiation tool, a large number of suppliers can sustain the process for a longer duration, giving more wide suppliers a better opportunity at winning the enterprise.

Communication with New Suppliers:

After informing the winning supplier(s), they should be invited to take part in executing recommendations. The execution plans vary according to the scale of switches the supplier makes. For obligatory purposes, a communication plan will be set up, including any modification in specifications and improvements in delivery, service, or pricing models. These tend to be communicated to users as well. As we know, the company gains immensely from this entire process of creating a communication plan, making some modifications according to the customer demand, and further forwarding this to the customer. It's essential that this process should be acknowledged by both the company and the supplier. For new suppliers, we need to construct a communication plan that copes with the alteration from old to new at every point in the process engaged by the spend category. The sections that have an impact on this change are the department, finance, and customer service. In addition, the risk antennae will be particularly sensitive during this period. It is essential to gauge closely the new supplier's performance during the first weeks of performance. Another essential task is to grasp the intellectual capital of the sourcing team, which has been developed within the seven-step process; so that it can be used the next time that category is sourced.

SM- MAKE VS BUY

Production units are identified mostly by their decision to make or buy. In other words, do they wish to produce the desired product on their own or do they want to purchase it from a foreign market? This decision is critical because the third-party suppliers especially in countries like Eastern Europe, China, and other low-cost parts of the world hold out the promise of essential beneficiaries, which the developed nations fail to offer. However, developed countries can easily overcome the expenses cost of the imported material through activities like human resources, information technology, maintenance, and customer relations. If properly utilized and taken care of, these activities may yield profit rather than leading the nation to suffer more losses. All the expense of outsourcing can be regained through these activities and thus they should not be neglected when the options are considered.

The Make Vs Buy decision of a nation depends on three pillars. These pillars are:

1. Business strategy
2. Risks
3. Economic factors

Business Strategy:

The first pillar in the Make Vs Buy decision is the business strategy adopted by a nation. Business strategystrategically engages the importance of the company whose product or service is being considered for outsourcing, in addition to the process, technologies, or skills needed to design the product or deliver that particular service. These factors should be carefully considered, not just on the basis of the current competitive environment but also by anticipating the changing competitive environment in the future. So, as a rule, it's advisable to select the in-house skills and abilities when a product or a function plays a very important role in improving the company's performance or is considered a core operation. Perhaps, if we consider a time-sensitive product or a product, which is prone to consequent design changes, third-party producing would likely be a mistake. In simple worlds, companies must opt for outsourcing in the following scenarios:

1. Remove the processes, which are intensive on the balance sheet, e.g., capital or labor.
2. Minimize the costs.

3. Achieve flexibility for adjusting output in comeback to changing demand.
4. Phase out the management of paperwork, documents or training.
5. Monitor fewer workers.
6. Have access to a new process or network tools and technologies.
7. Leverage external expertise.

In fact, if a product relies on proprietary technology or intellectual property or if a product or an operation is critical for the company's performance, it is recommended to select in-house skills & abilities rather than outsourcing. Obviously, outsourcing is worth considering in some situations. If a product or function has essentially become a commodity or is derived from factors other than unique or differentiating capabilities and as such, moving production or management to a third party does not give rise to significant risk to the company's strategy, outsourcing would be the perfect solution.

Risks:

The second pillarunder the Make Vs Buy strategy is the risksinvolved with any decision. The major risk factors involved in making a product in the home country or purchasing it from foreign countries are quality, reliability, and predictability of outsourced solutions or services. Along with these, there are risks inherent in the process of labeling and selecting the right supplier and structuring a workable ongoing relationship. When we have numerous suppliers, a single failure in the supply chain may not be deadly. Even when the suppliers are making parts of an item instead of that completely furnished item, there will be errors in manufacturing. These errors should be identified before the products are assembled so that the faulty item cannot be delivered to the consumer directly.

We know outsourcing opens up a broad array of new risks. We need to be attentive to any potential pitfalls with producers and examine outsourcing partners on the basis of their importance to the company. Operations in outsourcing that lead to failure of service could be overwhelming, for example, an IT network, a payroll processing system, or element manufacturing, as compared to risks or problems like a glitch in a training program or a long-term product development plan, which is much lesser. It is very important to acknowledge the risks that are related to the location of an external supplier. Apart from judging the source country's political stability, companies require to examine the safety and lead times of shipment schedules. Along with this, they have to label and examine potential secondary carriers or routes or search for other producers as a backup in a different area that supplies incremental volume during peaks in demand or disruptions of the primary source of supply.

When we merge the outsourced manufacturing of products or outsourced processes that demand distinct skills or assets, making it difficult or expensive to re-source, supply chain management becomes a highly complex function. In fact, these risks through which a producer may exploit a customer's highly reliable relationship by increasing prices or charging better terms (referred to as hold up risks) can be easily handled with some external solutions.

Economic Factors:

The **third pillar** in the Make Vs Buy strategy is the **economic factors** residing in the country that needs to decide if to buy a product or make it on its own. The various economic factors comprise the effect of outsourcing on capital expenditures, return on invested capital and return on assets, along with the probable savings gained by outsourcing.

To study the importance of pricing mechanisms, let's consider those companies that base their decision on if they need to outsource solely on approximate calculations of the in house as compared to the external costs related to the outsourced function.

For example, the cost of each item produced or the price of running an HR department or an IT network instead on the total costs. The net prices that need to be taken care of comprise the layouts for handling the outsource supplier, exclusively as the outsourced process changes. These changes prove to be very essential.

For example, customizing some software on a third-party information technology network can compute a large surcharge to the outsourcing deal. Tackling the customization in-house, i.e., within the home country, where the IT department can work closely, their work can be easily monitored and more productively with end-users to satisfy their demands can be obtained, tend to be less costly.

Along with this, the home country needs to choose the outsourcing partners very cautiously. In case the outsourcing partners are not selected properly, the companies often attempt to protect themselves from failures or delays by replicating in-house some of the effort that was originally farmed out. This leads to multiple prices for the same project and potential costs are mostly neglected when the outsourcing deal is made.

The costs that are often neglected in outsourcing manufacturing operations are as follows:

1. Transportation and handling charges.
2. Expanded, extended inventories.
3. Administrative bills like the supplier management and quality control rates.
4. Casted complexity and its effect on lean flows.
5. Minimal return on invested capital.
6. Production dependability and quality control.

Taking all these costs into consideration, depending on a one-time quote to measure the competitiveness of an external producer is mostly not enough. Enterprises can be saved from this mistake by factoring into the outsourcing equation the economic effects of comparative wage prices, labor productivity, tools and staff utilization, the biasness of both the labor base and functional processes, the potential for process and product innovation and relative purchasing power. Finally, we can say that for a successful outsourcing relationship, the basic factors include the sharing of savings from productivity progress, so that both sides have an inducement to merge.

After establishing a sober formal relationship, it is very essential to search for the right balance between fully transparent supplier functions and micromanagement or the perception of it. After the outsourcing decisions are made and suppliers have been chosen, it is crucial to be on the same front on a fair and balanced pricing mechanism, productivity progress and cost minimization expectations and the necessary scale of responsiveness to design, service or delivery changes.

SCM: NETWORKS:

The network design in supply chain determines its physical arrangement, design, structural layout and infrastructure of the supply chain. Here the major decisions to be made are on the number, locations and size of manufacturing plants and warehouses and the assignment of retail outlets to warehouses, etc. This stage witnesses some other major sourcing decisions as well. The basic time duration for planning horizon is few years. Many major decisions involving the long-term location, capacity, technology and supplier selection have to be made by considering the probable uncertainties present in the market development accompanied by changing economic and legal conditions.

Supply Chain Management: The network design in supply chain concentrates mainly on the development of multistage stochastic optimization methods required for decision support under demand, freight rate and exchange rate uncertainty. Here, we will discuss the various strategies to study the uncertainty and scenario modeling.

Warehouse location: When companies expand their branches into various new locations, they need new storage places as well. Here the company faces a warehouse location problem. Within the set of probable choices in locations, the one that has minimal fixed costs and operational costs by fulfilling the required demand is chosen.

Traffic network design: With the growing population, the traffic in cities is increasing. Because of the higher transportation demand, the traffic networks have also to be widened. Since the budget allotted is usually limited, the major issue is to determine which projects should be constructed to develop the flow inside a traffic network.

Restoring: This phenomenon has emerged recently because of the rising cost and other circumstances. It is the exercise of bringing outsourced products and services back to the source point from which they were originally shipped. It outlines the process of moving some or all producing back to its original source.

NETWORK MODELS

Supply chain networks present different types of models that help us understand the various optimization methods used for studying uncertainty and scenario modelling. There are six distinct supply chain network models, as given below.

- Producer storage with direct shipping
- Producer storage with direct shipping and in-transit merge (cross docking)
- Distributor storage with package carrier delivery
- Distributor storage with last mile delivery
- Producer or distributor storage with costumer pickup
- Retail storage with customer pickup

The supply chain network basically deals with three major entities: Producer, Distributor, and Merchant. Two different options are available, i.e., customer pickup or door delivery. For example, if the door delivery option is opted for, there is transport between producer and distributor, distributor and merchant and producer and merchant. The distribution system decision is made on the basis of the choice of the customers. This in turn results in the demand for the product or products and the cost of the distribution arrangement. New companies may come to a halt through the application of a single type of distribution network. Mostly, companies go for merging different types for distinct products, different customers and different usage situations, coming back to the different optimization models mentioned above. Now we will discuss each model in brief.

Producer Storage with Direct Shipping:

In this model, goods are moved directly from the manufacturer's location as the starting point to the end customer's location as the destination point bypassing the retailer. The retailer is the person who takes the order and initiates the delivery request. This option of Supply Chain Management is also called drop-shipping, with products delivered directly from the manufacturer's location to the customer's destination.

Producer Storage with Direct Shipping and In-Transit Merge:

It is somewhat congruent to pure drop-shipping or moving, but the difference is that pieces of the order come from different locations and they are merged into one so that the customer gets a single delivery.

Distributor Storage with Package Carrier Delivery:

This comes into action when the inventory is not owned by the manufacturers at the plants; instead, it is owned by the merchants/retailers in intermediate warehouses and package carriers are used for the shipment of goods from the intermediate location to the final customer.

Distributor Storage with Last Mile Delivery:

This type results when the merchant/retailer delivers the goods ordered by the customer to the customer's home instead of using a package carrier.

SCM- INVENTORY MANAGEMENT

Producer/distributor storage with customer pickup

In this type, the inventory is stored at the warehouse owned by the manufacturer or producer but the customers place their orders online or by phone and then come to pick up points allotted for collecting their orders.

Retail Storage with Customer Pickup:

This is mostly applied in situations when inventory is locally stored at retail stores; customers walk into the retail shop or order something online or on the phone and pick it up at the retail store. As seen under the major objectives of the supply chain, one of the basic objectives of SCM is to make sure that all the activities and functions within as well as across the company are managed efficiently. There are instances where efficiency in the supply chain can be ensured by efficiencies in inventory, to be more precise, by maintaining efficiency in inventory reductions. Though inventory is considered a liability to efficient supply chain management, supply chain managers acknowledge the need for inventory. However, the unwritten rule is to keep inventory at a bare minimum.

Many strategies are developed with the objective of streamlining inventories beyond the supply chain and holding the inventory investment as low as possible. The supply chain managers tend to maintain the inventories as low as possible because of inventory investment. The cost or investment related to owning inventories can be high. These costs comprise the cash outlay that is necessary for purchasing the inventory, the costs of acquiring the inventories (the cost of having invested in inventories rather than investing in something else), and the costs related to managing the inventory.

Role of Inventory

Before understanding the role of inventory in supply chain, we need to understand the cordial relationship between the manufacturer and the client. Handling clients, coping with their demands, and creating relationships with manufacturers is a critical sections of managing supply chains. There are many instances where we see the concept of the collaborative relationship being marked as the essence of supply chain management. However, a deeper analysis of supply chain relationships, especially those including product flows, exposes that at the heart of these relationships is inventory movement and storage. More than half of it relies on the purchase, transfer, or management of inventory. As we know, inventory plays a very important role in supply chains, being a salient feature.

The most fundamental functions that inventory has in supply chains are as follows:

1. To supply and support the balance of demand and supply.
2. To effectively cope with the forward and reverse flows in the supply chain.

Companies need to manage the upstream supplier exchanges and downstream customer demands. In this situation, the company enters a state where it has to maintain a balance between fulfilling the demands of customers, which is mostly very difficult to predict with precision or accuracy, and maintaining an adequate supply of materials and goods. This balance can be obtained through inventory.

MRS. POORNIMA G, ASSISTANT PROFESSOR IN COMMERCE, A J K
COLLEGE OF ARTS AND SCIENCE COIMBATORE

OPTIMIZATION MODELS

Optimization models of supply chain are those models that codify practical or real life issues into mathematical model. The main objective to construct this mathematical model is to maximize or minimize an objective function. In addition to this, some constraints are added to these issues for defining the feasible region. We try to generate an efficient algorithm that will examine all possible solutions and return the best solution in the end. Various supply chain optimization models are as follows:

Mixed Integer Linear Programming:

The Mixed integer linear programming (MILP) is a mathematical modeling approach used to get the best outcome of a system with some restrictions. This model is broadly used in many optimization areas such as production planning, transportation, network design, etc. MILP comprises a linear objective function along with some limitation constraints constructed by continuous and integer variables. The main objective of this model is to get an optimal solution of the objective function. This may be the maximum or minimum value but it should be achieved without violating any of the constraints imposed. We can say that MILP is a special case of linear programming that uses binary variables. When compared with normal linear programming models, they are slightly tough to solve. Basically the MILP models are solved by commercial and non-commercial solvers, **for example:** Fico Xpress or SCIP.

Stochastic Modeling:

Stochastic modeling is a mathematical approach of representing data or predicting outcomes in situations where there is randomness or unpredictability to some extent. For example, in a production unit, the manufacturing process generally has some unknown parameters like quality of the input materials, reliability of the machines and competence within the employees. These parameters have an impact on the outcome of the manufacturing process but it is impossible to measure them with absolute values. In these types of cases, where we need to find absolute value for unknown parameters, which cannot be measured exactly, we use Stochastic modeling approach. This modeling strategy helps in predicting the result of this process with some defined error rate by considering the unpredictability of these factors.

Uncertainty Modeling:

While using a realistic modeling approach, the system has to take uncertainties into account. The uncertainty is evaluated to a level where the uncertain characteristics of the system are modeled with probabilistic nature. We use uncertainty modeling for characterizing the uncertain parameters with probability distributions. It takes dependencies into account easily as input just like Markov chain or may use the queuing theory for modeling the systems where waiting has an essential role. These are common ways of modeling uncertainty.

Bi-level Optimization:

A bi-level issue arises in real-life situations whenever a decentralized or hierarchical decision needs to be made. In these types of situations, multiple parties make decisions one after the other, which influences their respective profit. Till now, the only solution to solve bi-level problems is through heuristic methods for realistic sizes. However, attempts are being made for improving these optimal methods to compute an optimal solution for real problems as well. Pricing is a factor that gears up profits in the supply chain through an appropriate match of supply and demand.

Revenue management can be defined as the application of pricing to increase the profit produced from a limited supply of supply chain assets. Ideas from revenue management recommend that a company should first use pricing to maintain a balance between supply and demand and should think of further investing or eliminating assets only after the balance is maintained.

The assets in supply chain are present in two forms, namely **capacity,** and **Inventory**.

Capacity assets in the supply chain are present for manufacturing, shipment, and storage while inventory assets are present within the supply chain and are carried to develop and improvise product availability. Thus, we can further define revenue management as the application of differential pricing on the basis of customer segment, time of use and product or capacity availability to increment supply chain surplus.

Process View of Supply Chain

- A supply chain is a sequence of processes and flows that take place within and between different stages and combine to fill a customer need for a product
- Two ways to view the processes performed in a supply chain Cycles view and Push/pull view

Cycle view

- Defines the processes involved and the owners of each process

- Process in a supply chain are divided into a series of cycles
- Cycles are performed at the interface between two successive stages of a supply chain
- Supply chain process can be broken down into four process cycles such as

1. Customer order cycle
2. Replenishment cycle
3. Manufacturing cycle
4. Procurement cycle

- Each cycles occurs at the interface between two successive stages of the supply chain
- A cycle view of the supply chain is very useful when considering operational decisions
- It clearly specifies the roles and responsibilities of each member of the supply chain
- It helps the designer to consider the infrastructure required to support the processes

COMPETITIVENESS AND SUPPLY CHAIN STRATEGIES

1. Competitive strategy of a company defines the set of customer needs that it seeks to satisfy through its products and services
2. Defined based on how customer prioritizes product cost, delivery time, variety and quality
3. Targets one or more customer segments and aims to provide products and services that satisfy these

customer's needs

4. Some company's competitive strategies are defined around the following

- High availability of a variety of reasonable quality products at low prices – e.g.: Wal-Mart
- Better customer convenience, availability and responsiveness – e.g.: McMaster Carr – MRO items - over 200,000 items through catalog and web site
- Better customization, and variety at reasonable cost – e.g.: Dell
- To execute a competitive strategy of a company, all the functions play a role and each must develop its own strategy
- Supply chain strategy determines
- the nature of procurement of raw materials,
- transportation of materials to and from the company,
- manufacture of the product or operations to provide the service, and
- distribution of the product to the customer, along with any follow-up service
- This strategy includes what many traditionally include

1. Supplier strategy
2. Operations strategy, and
3. Logistics strategy
4. Decisions regarding inventory, operating facilities, transportation, and information flows in the supply chain are all part of the supply chain strategy

Achieving Strategic Fit

1. Strategic fit means that both the competitive and supply chain strategies have the same goal
2. It refers to consistency between
3. The customer priorities that the competitive strategy hopes to satisfy and
4. The supply chain capabilities that the supply chain strategy aims to build
5. Major task of the chief executive officer (CEO) is aligning all of the core strategies with the overall competitive strategy to achieve strategic fit
6. During the supply chain design a key consideration is the strategic fit
7. A company's success or failure is closely linked to the following

- The competitive strategy and all functional strategies must fit together to form a coordinated overall strategy
- Different functions in a company must appropriately structure their process and resources to be able to execute these strategies successfully

Understanding the Customer and Supply Chain Uncertainty

- To understand the customer, a company must identify the needs of the customer segment being served
- Customer demand from different segments may vary along several attributes:

1. The quantity of the product needed in each lot

2. The response time that customers are willing to tolerate
3. The variety of products needed
4. The service level required
5. The price of the product
6. The desired rate of innovation in the product

Implied Demand Uncertainty

- Demand uncertainty reflects the uncertainty of customer demand for the product
- Implied demand uncertainty is the uncertainty in meeting a portion of customer demand and it is the uncertainty the supply chain faces.
- It is mainly due to the attributes the customer desires
Illustration

As a supply chain raises its service level, it must be able to meet a higher and higher percentage of actual demand, forcing it to prepare for rare surges in demand. Thus raising the service level increases the implied demand uncertainty even though the product's underlying demand uncertainty does not change.

- Product demand uncertainty and various customer needs that the supply chain tries to fill affect implied demand uncertainty

The following customer needs increase implied demand uncertainty

- Range quantity required increases
- Lead time decreases

- Variety of products required increases
- Number of channels through which the product may be acquired increases
- Rate of innovation increases
- Required service level increases

Multiple Products and Customer Segments

- Firms often sells multiple products and serves customer segments with very different needs
- Different products and segments have different implied demand uncertainty
- Key issue for company is to create a supply chain that balances efficiency and responsiveness given its portfolio of products, customer segments, and supply sources
- Several possible routes a company can take
- One route – set up independent supply chains for each different product or customer segment Feasible if each segment is large enough to support a dedicated supply chain
- Preferable strategy is to tailor the supply chain to best meet the needs of each product's demand Tailoring the supply chain requires some links in the supply chain with some products, while having separate operations for other links – considering efficiency and responsiveness.

PRODUCT LIFE CYCLE

- As product go through their life cycle, the demand characteristics and the needs of the customer segments being served change
- As product mature, the corresponding supply chain strategy should, in general, move from being responsive to being efficient
- Competitor can change the landscape of the market
- Growth of mass customization – competitors flood the marketplace with product variety, customers are becoming accustomed to having their individual needs satisfied
- Competitive focus today is on producing sufficient variety at a reasonable price
- As competitive landscape changes, a firm is forced to alter its competitive strategy –resulting in change in supply chain strategy

EXPANDING STRATEGIC SCOPE

- Scope of strategic fit refers to the function and stages that devices an integrated strategy with a shared objective
- One extreme - operation within a function devices independent strategy
- Other extreme - all functional areas within all stages of the supply chain device strategy jointly with a common objective

Intercompany Interoperation Scope: Minimizes Local Cost View

- Strategic fit is considered in one operation within a functional area within a company
- Resulting collection of strategies will most likely not come close to maximizing supply chain profit – conflicting local objectives
- Practices during 1950s and 1960s

Intercompany Intrafunctional Scope: Minimize Functional Cost View

- Given that many operations together form each function within a firm, managers recognized the weakness of the intercompany interoperation scope
- With the intercompany intrafunction scope, the strategic fit is expanded to include all operations within a function
- The scope of strategic fit expands to an entire function within a stage of the supply chain

An example of intercompany intrafunctional scope of supply chain strategy at a distributor

Intercompany interfunctional scope: maximize company profit view

- Different functions may have conflicting objectives
- Functional strategies are developed to support both each other and the competitive strategy Intercompany interfunctional scope: maximized supply chain surplus view
- Intercompany interfunctional scope leads to each stage of the supply chain trying to maximized its own profits, which does not necessarily result in the maximization of supply chain surplus

- When company uses speed as their primary competitive advantage to succeed in the marketplace, intercompany interfunctional strategy performs badly

The impediment to create level of speed that customers are demanding lies to a degree within their own boundaries

Managing these interfaces becomes a key to providing speed to customers

- Intercompany scope forces every stage of the supply chain to look across the supply chain and evaluate the impact of its action on other stages as well as on the interfaces
- This means treating stages in the supply chain that a company does not own as belonging to the company.

The intercompany interfunctional scope of strategic fit Agile intercompany interfunctional scope

- Till now the discussion was on strategic fit under static context – players in supply chain and customers do not change over time
- Dynamics exits – product life cycle get shorter and companies try to satisfy the changing needs of individual customers
- In such situations, a company may have to partner with many different firms depending on the product being produced and the customer being served strategic fit should have agile intercompany scope.

SCM- INVENTORY MANAGEMENT:

Inventory Management of Supply Chain Management:
Inventory management, a critical element of the supply chain, is the tracking of inventory from manufacturers to warehouses and from these facilities to a point of sale. The goal of inventory management is to have the right products in the right place at the right time.

Producer/Distributor Storage with Customer Pickup:
In this type, the inventory is stored at the warehouse owned by the manufacturer or producer but the customers place their orders online or through phone and then come to pick up points allotted for collecting their orders.

Retail Storage with Customer Pickup:
This is mostly applied on situations when inventory is locally stored at retail stores; customers walk into the retail shop or order something online or on the phone and pick it up at the retail store.

As seen under the major objectives of supply chain, one of the basic objectives of SCM is to make sure that all the activities and functions within as well as across the company are managed efficiently.

There are instances where efficiency in supply chain can be ensured by efficiencies in inventory, to be more precise, by maintaining efficiency in inventory reductions. Though inventory is considered a liability to efficient supply chain management, supply chain managers acknowledge the need of inventory. However, the unwritten rule is to keep inventory at a bare minimum.

Many strategies are developed with the objective of streamlining inventories beyond the supply chain and holding the inventory investment as low as possible. The supply chain managers tend to maintain the inventories as low as possible because of inventory investment. The cost or investment related with owning inventories can be high. These costs comprise the cash outlay that is necessary for purchasing the inventory, the costs of acquiring the inventories (the cost of having invested in inventories rather than investing in something else) and the costs related with managing the inventory.

Role of Inventory

Before understanding the role of inventory in supply chain, we need to understand the cordial relationship between the manufacturer and the client. Handling clients, coping up with their demands and creating relationships with manufacturer is a critical section of managing supply chains. There are many instances where we see the concept of collaborative relationship being marked as the essence of supply chain management. However, a deeper analysis of supply chain relationships, especially those including product flows, exposes that at the heart of these relationships is inventory movement and storage. More than half of it relies on the purchase, transfer or management of inventory. As we know, inventory plays a very important role in supply chains, being a salient feature.

The most fundamental functions that inventory has in supply chains are as follows:

To supply and support the balance of demand and supply.
To effectively cope with the forward and reverse flows in the supply chain.

Companies need to manage the upstream supplier exchanges and downstream customer demands. In this situation, the company enters a state where it has to maintain a balance between fulfilling the demands of customers, which is mostly very difficult to predict with precision or accuracy, and maintaining adequate supply of materials and goods. This balance can be obtained through inventory.

SCM- PRICING & REVENUE MANAGEMENT

Revenue management plays a major role in supply chain and has a share of credit in the profitability of supply chain when one or more of the following conditions exist:

1. The product value differs in different market segments
2. The product is highly perishable or product tends to be defective.
3. Demand has seasonal and other peaks.
4. The product is sold both in bulk and the spot market.

The strategy of revenue management has been successfully applied in many streams that we often tend to use but it is never noticed. For example, the finest real life application of revenue management can be seen in the airline, railway, hotel and resort, cruise ship, healthcare, printing and publishing.

RM for Multiple Customer Segments

In the concept of revenue management, we need to take care of two fundamental issues. The first one is how to distinguish between two segments and design their pricing to make one segment pay more than the other. Secondly, how to control the demand so that the lower price segment does not use the complete asset that is available.

To gain completely from revenue management, the manufacturer needs to minimize the volume of capacity devoted to lower price segment even if enough demand is available from the lower price segment to utilize the complete volume. Here, the general trade-off is in between placing an order from a lower price or waiting for a high price to arrive later on.

These types of situations invite risks like spoilage and spill. Spoilage appears when volumes of goods are wasted due to demand from high rate that does not materialize. Similarly, spill appears if higher rate segments need to be rejected due to the commitment of volume goods given to the lower price segment.

Supply Chain Management

To reduce the cost of spoilage and spill, the manufacturer can apply the formula given below to segments. Let us assume that the anticipated demand for the higher price segment is generally distributed with mean of DH and standard deviation of σH:

$$CH = F^{-1}(1\text{-}pL/pH, DH, \sigma H) = NORMINV\ (1\text{-}pL/pH, DH, \sigma H)$$

Where,

CH = reserve capacity for higher price segment pL = the price for lower segment pH = the price for higher segment

An important point to note here is the application of differential pricing that increments the level of asset availability for the high price segment. A different approach that is applicable for differential pricing is to build multiple versions of product that focus on different segments. We can understand this concept with the help of a real life application of managing revenue for multiple customer segments, that is, the airlines.

RM for Perishable Assets:

Any asset that loses its value in due course of time is considered as a perishable item, for example, all fruits, vegetables and pharmaceuticals. We can also include computers, cell phones, fashion apparels, etc.; whatever loses its value after the launch of new model is considered as perishable.

We use two approaches for perishable assets in the revenue management. These approaches are:

- Fluctuate cost over time to maximize expected revenue.
- Overbook sales of the assets to cope or deal with cancellations.

The first approach is highly recommended for goods like fashion apparels that have a precise date across which they lose a lot of their value; for example, apparel designed for particular season doesn't have much value in the end of the season. The manufacturer should try using effective pricing strategy and predict the effect of rate on customer demand to increase total profit. Here the general trade-off is to demand high price initially and allow the remaining products to be sold later at lower price. The alternate method may be charging lower price initially, selling more products early in the season and then leaving fewer products to be sold at a discount. The second approach is very fruitful here. There are occurrences where the clients are able to cancel placed orders and the value of asset lowers significantly after the deadline.

RM for Seasonal Demands:

One of the major applications of revenue management can be seen in the seasonal demand. Here we see a demand shift from the peak to the off-peak duration; hence a better balance can be maintained between supply and demand. It also generates higher overall profit.

The commonly used effective and efficient revenue management approach to cope with seasonal demand is to demand higher price during peak time duration and a lower price during off-peak time duration. This approach leads to transferring demand from peak to off-peak period.

Companies offer discounts and other value-added services to motivate and allure customers to move their demand to off-peak period. The best suited example is Amazon.com. Amazon has a peak period in December, as it brings short-term volume that is expensive and reduces the profit margin. It tempts customers through various discounts and free shipping for orders that are placed in the month of November.

This approach of reducing and increasing the price according to the demand of customers in the peak season generates a higher profit for various companies just like it does for Amazon.com.

RM for Bulk and Spot Demands

When we talk about managing revenue for bulk and spot demand, the basic trade-off is somewhat congruent to that of revenue management for multiple customer segments.

The company has to make a decision regarding the quantity of asset to be booked for spot market, which is higher price. The booked quantity will depend upon the differences in order between the spot market and the bulk sale, along with the distribution of demand from the spot market.

There is a similar situation for the client who tends to make the buying decision for production, warehousing and transportation assets. Here the basic tradeoff is between signing on long-term bulk agreement with a fixed, lower price that can be wasted if not used and buying in the spot market with higher price that can never be wasted. The basic decision to be made here is the size of the bulk contract.

A formula that can be applied to achieve optimal amount of the asset to be purchased in bulk is given below. If demand is normal with mean μ and standard deviation σ, the optimal amount Q* to be purchased in bulk is

$Q^* = F^{-1}\,(p^*, \mu, \sigma) = NORMINV\,(p^*, \mu, \sigma)$

Where, p* = probability demand for the asset doesn't exceed Q*

Q* = the optimal amount of the asset to be purchased in bulk

The amount of bulk purchase increases if either the spot market price increases or the bulk price decreases. We can now conclude that revenue management is nothing but application of differential pricing on the basis of customer segments, time of use, and product or capacity availability to increase supply chain profit. It comprises marketing, finance, and operation functions to maximize the net profit earned.

Supply chain integration can be defined as a close calibration and collaboration within a supply chain, mostly with the application of shared management information systems. A supply chain is made from all parties that participate in the completion of a purchase, like the resources, raw materials, manufacturing of the product, shipping of completed products and facilitating services.

There are different levels of supply chain integration. We will understand this with the help of an example of a computer manufacturing company. The initial step in integration shall include choosing precise merchants to supply certain inputs and ensuring compliance for them for supplying certain amount of inputs within the year at a set cost.

This assures that the company has the appropriate materials required to produce the expected output of computers during the year. In the meanwhile, this computer company may sign a bond with a large supplier of circuit boards; the bond expects it to deliver a precise quantity at precise times within a year and fix a price that will be effective during the bond year.

If we move to a higher level, the next step would be to integrate the companies more closely. The circuit board supplier may construct a plant close to the assembly plant and may also share production software. Hence, the circuit board company would be able to see how many boards are required in the upcoming month and can construct them in time, as the company requires them in order to meet its sales demand.

Benefits of Inventory Management

The two main benefits of inventory management are that it ensures you're able to fulfill incoming or open orders and raises profits. Inventory management also:

Saves Money: Understanding stock trends means you see how much of and where you have something in stock so you're better able to use the stock you have. This also allows you to keep less stock at each location (store, warehouse), as you're able to pull from anywhere to fulfill orders all of this decreases costs tied up in inventory and decreases the amount of stock that goes unsold before it obsolete.

Improves Cash Flow: With proper inventory management, you spend money on inventory that sells, so cash is always moving through the business.

Satisfies Customers: One element of developing loyal customers is ensuring they receive the items they want without waiting. Inventory Management Challenges. The primary challenges of inventory management are having too much inventory and not being able to sell it, not having enough inventory to fulfill orders, and not understanding what items you have in inventory and where they're located. Other obstacles include.

Getting Accurate Stock Details: If you don't have accurate stock details, there's no way to know when to refill stock or which stock moves well.

Poor Processes: Outdated or manual processes can make work error-prone and slow down operations.

Changing Customer Demand Customer tastes and needs change constantly. If your system can't track trends, how will you know when their preferences change and why?

Using Warehouse Space Well: Staff wastes time if like products is hard to locate. Mastering inventory management can help eliminate this challenge.

What Is Inventory?

Inventory is the raw materials, components, and finished goods a company sells or uses in production. Accounting considers inventory an asset. Accountants use the information about stock levels to record the correct valuations on the balance sheet.

Inventory vs. Stock

Inventory is often called stock in retail businesses: Managers frequently use the term "stock on hand" to refer to products like apparel and housewares. Across industries, "inventory" more broadly refers to stored sales goods and raw materials and parts used in production.

Some people also say that the word "stock" is used more commonly in the U.K. to refer to inventory. While there is a difference between the two, the terms inventory and stock are often interchangeable.

What Are the Different Types of Inventory?

There are 12 different types of inventory: raw materials, work-in-progress (WIP), finished goods, decoupling inventory, safety stock, packing materials, cycle inventory, service inventory, transit, theoretical, excess and maintenance, repair and operations (MRO). Some people do not recognize MRO as a type of inventory.

Inventory Management Process

If you produce on demand, the inventory management process starts when a company receives a customer order and continues until the order ships. Otherwise, the process begins when you forecast your demand and then place POs for the required raw materials or components. Other parts of the process include analyzing sales trends and organizing the storage of products in warehouses.

How Inventory Management Works

The goal of inventory management is to understand stock levels and stock's location in warehouses. Inventory management software tracks the flow of products from supplier through the production process to the customer. In the warehouse, inventory management tracks stock receipt, picking, packing and shipping.

Inventory Management Techniques and Terms

Some inventory management techniques use formulas and analysis to plan stock. Others rely on procedures. All methods aim to improve accuracy. The techniques a company uses depend on its needs and stock. Find out which technique works best for your business by reading the guide to inventory management techniques. Here's a summary of them:

ABC Analysis: This method works by identifying the most and least popular types of stock.

Batch Tracking: This method groups similar items to track expiration dates and trace defective items.

Bulk Shipments: This method considers unpacked materials that suppliers load directly into ships or trucks. It involves buying, storing and shipping inventory in bulk.

Consignment: When practicing consignment inventory management, your business won't pay its supplier until a given product is sold. That supplier also retains ownership of the inventory until your company sells it.

Cross-Docking: Using this method, you'll unload items directly from a supplier truck to the delivery truck. Warehousing is essentially eliminated.

Demand Forecasting: This form of predictive analytics helps predict customer demand.

Dropshipping: In this practice, the supplier ships items directly from its warehouse to the customer.

Economic Order Quantity (EOQ): This formula shows exactly how much inventory a company should order to reduce holding and other costs.

FIFO and LIFO: First in, first out (FIFO) means you move the oldest stock first. Last in, first out (LIFO) considers that prices always rise, so the most recently-purchased inventory is the most expensive and thus sold first.

Just-In-Time Inventory (JIT): Companies use this method in an effort to maintain the lowest stock levels possible before a refill.

Lean Manufacturing: This methodology focuses on removing waste or any item that does not provide value to the customer from the manufacturing system.

Materials Requirements Planning (MRP): This system handles planning, scheduling and inventory control for manufacturing.

Minimum Order Quantity: A company that relies on minimum order quantity will order minimum amounts of inventory from wholesalers in each order to keep costs low.

Reorder Point Formula: Businesses use this formula to find the minimum amount of stock they should have before reordering, then manage their inventory accordingly.

Perpetual Inventory Management: This technique entails recording stock sales and usage in real-time. Read "The Definitive Guide toPerpetual Inventory" to learn more about this practice.

Safety Stock: An inventory management ethos that prioritizes safety stock will ensure there's always extra stock set aside in case the company can't replenish those items.

Six Sigma: This is a data-based method for removing waste from businesses as it relates to inventory.

Lean Six Sigma: This method combines lean management and Six Sigma practices to remove waste and raise efficiency.

Inventory vs. Cycle Counting

"Taking inventory" is the process of physically counting all stock, once a year in most cases. Cycle counting is the practice of counting a selected set of stock more often. Cycle counting serves as an important means of checks and balances to ensure the amount of inventory represented in the inventory management system is what you have on the shelf. A cycle counting best practice is to count specific SKUs regularly and integrate it into the daily tasks of warehouse staff. Companies may determine different standards for different types of inventory, such as performing a cycle count of top-moving SKUs or higher-value items. Learn more about the benefits of cycle counting.

Demand Planning and Inventory Management:
Demand planning is an important part of successful inventory management. It is the process of determining how much of each item you anticipate selling, and when. Once demand is determined, inventory management follows the flow of goods from the supplier through production and ultimately fulfilling customer orders. Find

out more about how demand planning and inventory management work together in the "Essential Guide to Inventory Planning."

Inventory Management Formulas

Understanding inventory management formulas are crucial to optimizing stock levels. Multiple inventory and accounting professionals have vetted formulas to make inventory calculations easier.

Inventory Management KPIs

Effective inventory management plays an important role throughout the supply chain. There are many key performance indicators for measuring inventory management succcss throughout the different organizations in the business. Understand which calculations return the most insight into your business processes is important. To learn more, see inventory managementKPIs.

SCM- PRICING & REVENUE MANAGEMENT

Revenue management plays a major role in supply chain and has a share of credit in the profitability of supply chain when one or more of the following conditions exist:

1. The product value differs in different market segments
2. The product is highly perishable or product tends to be defective.
3. Demand has seasonal and other peaks.

4. The product is sold both in bulk and the spot market.

The strategy of revenue management has been successfully applied in many streams that we often tend to use but it is never noticed. For example, the finest real life application of revenue management can be seen in the airline, railway, hotel and resort, cruise ship, healthcare, printing and publishing.

RM for Multiple Customer Segments

In the concept of revenue management, we need to take care of two fundamental issues. The first one is how to distinguish between two segments and design their pricing to make one segment pay more than the other. Secondly, how to control the demand so that the lower price segment does not use the complete asset that is available.

To gain completely from revenue management, the manufacturer needs to minimize the volume of capacity devoted to lower price segment even if enough demand is available from the lower price segment to utilize the complete volume. Here, the general trade-off is in between placing an order from a lower price or waiting for a high price to arrive later on.

These types of situations invite risks like spoilage and spill. Spoilage appears when volumes of goods are wasted due to demand from high rate that does not materialize. Similarly, spill appears if higher rate segments need to be rejected due to the commitment of volume goods given to the lower price segment.

Supply Chain Management

To reduce the cost of spoilage and spill, the manufacturer can apply the formula given below to segments. Let us assume that the anticipated demand for the higher price segment is generally distributed with mean of DH and standard deviation of σH:

$$CH = F^{-1}(1-pL/pH, DH, \sigma H) = NORMINV\ (1-pL/pH, DH, \sigma H)$$

Where,

CH = reserve capacity for higher price segment pL = the price for lower segment pH = the price for higher segment

An important point to note here is the application of differential pricing that increments the level of asset availability for the high price segment. A different approach that is applicable for differential pricing is to build multiple versions of product that focus on different segments. We can understand this concept with the help of a real life application of managing revenue for multiple customer segments, that is, the airlines.

RM for Perishable Assets

Any asset that loses its value in due course of time is considered as a perishable item, for example, all fruits, vegetables and pharmaceuticals. We can also include computers, cell phones, fashion apparels, etc.; whatever loses its value after the launch of new model is considered as perishable.

We use two approaches for perishable assets in the revenue management. These approaches are:

- Fluctuate cost over time to maximize expected revenue.

- Overbook sales of the assets to cope or deal with cancellations.

The first approach is highly recommended for goods like fashion apparels that have a precise date across which they lose a lot of their value; for example, apparel designed for particular season doesn't have much value in the end of the season. The manufacturer should try using effective pricing strategy and predict the effect of rate on customer demand to increase total profit. Here the general trade-off is to demand high price initially and allow the remaining products to be sold later at lower price. The alternate method may be charging lower price initially, selling more products early in the season and then leaving fewer products to be sold at a discount.

The second approach is very fruitful here. There are occurrences where the clients are able to cancel placed orders and the value of asset lowers significantly after the deadline.

RM for Seasonal Demands:

One of the major applications of revenue management can be seen in the seasonal demand. Here we see a demand shift from the peak to the off-peak duration; hence a better balance can be maintained between supply and demand. It also generates higher overall profit.

The commonly used effective and efficient revenue management approach to cope with seasonal demand is to demand higher price during peak time duration and a lower price during off-peak time duration. This approach leads to transferring demand from peak to off-peak period.

Companies offer discounts and other value-added services to motivate and allure customers to move their demand to off-peak period. The best suited example is

Amazon.com. Amazon has a peak period in December, as it brings short-term volume that is expensive and reduces the profit margin. It tempts customers through various discounts and free shipping for orders that are placed in the month of November.

This approach of reducing and increasing the price according to the demand of customers in the peak season generates a higher profit for various companies just like it does for Amazon.com.

RM for Bulk and Spot Demands:

When we talk about managing revenue for bulk and spot demand, the basic trade-off is somewhat congruent to that of revenue management for multiple customer segments.

The company has to make a decision regarding the quantity of asset to be booked for spot market, which is higher price. The booked quantity will depend upon the differences in order between the spot market and the bulk sale, along with the distribution of demand from the spot market.

There is a similar situation for the client who tends to make the buying decision for production, warehousing and transportation assets. Here the basic tradeoff is between signing on long-term bulk agreement with a fixed, lower price that can be wasted if not used and buying in the spot market with higher price that can never be wasted. The basic decision to be made here is the size of the bulk contract.

A formula that can be applied to achieve optimal amount of the asset to be purchased in bulk is given below. If demand is normal with mean μ and standard deviation σ, the optimal amount Q^* to be purchased in bulk is

$$Q^* = F^{-1}(p^*, \mu, \sigma) = NORMINV(p^*, \mu, \sigma)$$

Where, p* = probability demand for the asset doesn't exceed Q*

Q* = the optimal amount of the asset to be purchased in bulk

The amount of bulk purchase increases if either the spot market price increases or the bulk price decreases. We can now conclude that revenue management is nothing but application of differential pricing on the basis of customer segments, time of use, and product or capacity availability to increase supply chain profit. It comprises marketing, finance, and operation functions to maximize the net profit earned.

Supply chain integration can be defined as a close calibration and collaboration within a supply chain, mostly with the application of shared management information systems. A supply chain is made from all parties that participate in the completion of a purchase, like the resources, raw materials, manufacturing of the product, shipping of completed products and facilitating services.

There are different levels of supply chain integration. We will understand this with the help of an example of a computer manufacturing company. The initial step in integration shall include choosing precise merchants to supply certain inputs and ensuring compliance for them for supplying certain amount of inputs within the year at a set cost.

This assures that the company has the appropriate materials required to produce the expected output of computers during the year. In the meanwhile, this computer company may sign a bond with a large supplier of circuit boards; the bond expects it to deliver a precise quantity at precise times within a year and fix a price that will be effective during the bond year.

If we move to a higher level, the next step would be to integrate the companies more closely. The circuit board supplier may construct a plant close to the assembly plant and may also share production software. Hence, the circuit board company would be able to see how many boards are

Required in the upcoming month and can construct them in time, as the company requires them in order to meet its sales demand.

Further higher level is referred as vertical integration. This level starts when the supply chain of a company is actually owned by the company itself. Here, a computer company may buy the circuit board company just to ensure a devoted supply of elements.

Economic Lot Size Model:

Economic Lot Size (ELS) was first dcvclopcd about 1913. It balances the costs of inventory against the costs of setup over a range of batch quantities. In this model, the Economic Lot Size (ELS) is where Total Cost is minimum. This model calculates the total production cost per unit over a range of batches.

Supply Contracts:

An agreement by which a seller promises to supply all of the specified goods or services that a buyer needs over a certain time and at a fixed price, and the buyer agrees to purchase such goods or services exclusively from the seller during that time The supply contract protects the rights of both parties.

A Supply Agreement is a document between two parties, a **Supplier,** and a **Purchaser**. The Supplier can be an individual or business and is the party that "**supplies,**" **or sells**, the **goods** to the Purchaser. The Purchaser can also be an individual or a business and is the party that **purchases for its use** the goods that the Supplier provides.

Supply chain contracts

Supply Chain Contracts are agreements that are deliberated and signed by the companies and the seller/producer/manufacturer which specify and hold either party responsible for their responsibilities on specifications which include and are not limited to: The method in which the payment will be made.

Five Key Provisions You Should Have in Your Supply-Chain Contracts

Protect your confidential information and company know-how: This helps you to maintain your competitive advantages. Achieving this in practice can be complicated, since it requires both practical and contractual protection. These are the features of strong confidential information protection in a supply-chain contract:

Clearly Define Confidential Information: Be sure to carefully detail exactly what comprises confidential information in your supplier contract. Consider including financial information, product pricing, business projections, designs, composites, moulds, tools, equipment, details of other suppliers, and any specialized processes, among other things.

Limit Access to any Confidential Information: This clause should outline the practical steps your supplier must take to prevent staff (or anyone else, including third-party vendors and subcontractors) from accessing your confidential information and know-how. These steps might include:

- Physical barriers,
- Restricted access to digital assets,
- Security measures,
- Having third parties agree to the confidentiality provision in your agreement (or similar confidentiality requirements),
- Assigning responsibility for maintaining confidentiality to a particular member of the supplier's team, and
- Ensuring that confidential information will be returned when the contract ends.

Detail who Owns any Intellectual Property Developed: Your supplier may develop I.P. while working on your project. The contract outlining your agreement should clearly assign rights to the I.P. to your company, if you wish to claim ownership of it.

Outline auditing procedures. Best practice means putting in effort far beyond the wording of the contract. You should have the ability to visit your suppliers' sites and review their records to ensure the measures required are in place and being adhered to. Your contract should outline how and when these audits may take place.

Detail your Materials and Quality Requirements. Diverse supply chains help to meet consumer expectations, grow profits, innovate, and stay competitive. They also make it more cumbersome to manage and guarantee quality. Clear and concise supplier contracts can help to mitigate materials and quality issues. Inclusion of a clause that details exact materials requirements can prevent suppliers from switching in lower-quality materials. You should outline the type, colour, shape, size, weight, and acceptable sources of the supplies.

As for quality requirements, your contract should outline a firm minimum standard for quality. You should specify the purpose of the product, and detail that the products delivered must be fit for purpose. Any quality-assurance tests required should be clear, as should the consequences of failing to meet the required standards.

Protect your I.P. from Counterfeits. The intellectual property law in any jurisdiction where you operate offers some protection from counterfeits, as long as you register your I.P. there. This protection can be amplified by liquidated damages provisions, which offer strong incentives for suppliers to protect your I.P., and provision for immediate injunctive relief where it's being infringed.

Liquidated damages provisions outline that, where your I.P. is being misused, sold, or "held hostage" during a dispute or following termination of the contract, your supplier will be required to pay you a predetermined sum of money.

An injunctive relief provision gives you the ability to legally require your supplier to stop doing whatever it is they're doing that contravenes the terms of your contract. In the context of I.P., your supplier would immediately need to stop selling the counterfeit products.

Non-approved third-party sales should also be covered in the liquidated damages clause. This prevents your supplier from selling off any excess products or products you reject. You can also achieve this by requiring your supplier to provide a third-party certification of destruction, or return your products to you.

Include conditions to promote contractual performance: The importance of carefully drafted performance clauses in your supply-chain contracts has never been more apparent than throughout the pandemic.

Court appearances, and the negotiation of settlements relating to non-performance during the pandemic, will continue for years to come.

Provisions that promote performance can be beneficial in these cases. These include:

- Performance guarantees from a parent company,
- Financial penalties for delays,
- Termination clauses for non-performance,
- Suspension or termination clauses for delayed performance,
- Escrow arrangements,
- Performance bonds, and
- Rights that allow another supplier to "step in" where the supplier has failed to deliver.

Plan for the end of your Contract: Supply-chain contracts should outline the circumstances under which parties can terminate a contract, and what happens once that termination occurs. You should be clear about what is owed to whom, and what steps must be taken both before and following termination.

Clear obligations from the outset minimize the risk of a dispute arising in the first place. If a termination occurs, it sets clear expectations for what's to follow — again, limiting the scope of any dispute. With these contractual protections and strong, strategic supply-chain relationships, you can better position your company for success in the future.

Centralized System:

In centralized organizations, strategic planning, goal setting, budgeting, and talent deployment are typically conducted by a single, senior leader or leadership team. In contrast, in decentralized organizations, formal decision-making power is distributed across multiple individuals or teams. A centralized supply chain is the traditional supply chain model, featuring a central headquarters and warehouse based in a single location. ... From a supply chain management standpoint, a centralized supply chain operation is typically managed at the headquarters – which handles all up and downstream decisions

Decentralized System:

Decentralization in an organization involves decision-making capability through middle management or lower management. Power, authority is upheld by lower management. In a decentralized supply chain, individual units make decisions based on local information. Such a system makes it easy to incentivize players to act in cooperation, making the entire supply chain efficient. ... A decentralized supply chain leads to higher cooperation over competition among entities in a supply chain.

Benefits of Centralized vs. Decentralized Systems in Supply Chain Management:

1. A centralized supply chain can help companies drive efficiencies through standardized processes.
2. A decentralized supply chain can empower individual sites to solve problems creatively.

Centralized supply chain: Visibility and process efficiency

For a global corporation with a large supplier base, centralizing supply chain operations makes sense. Business units might be separated not only by geography, but by different ERP systems, metrics or priorities. All this fragmentation obscures visibility into what's really going on and makes reducing costs, managing spend and achieving operational efficiencies more difficult. The right supply chain management software centralizes a supply chain by connecting current ERP systems seamlessly and acting as a central repository of data so that all locations speak the same language. In combination with built-in collaboration tools, a unified data model allows teams to work together and effectively mitigate potential risks.

Decentralized supply chains: Flexibility and agility for localized issues

At the same time, a completely centralized supply chain may not account for unique regional factors that affect supply and production.

Local managers need to be able to spot and adjust to changing market conditions on the ground. It might not always be feasible to do that in a highly centralized system if the decision- making authority is a couple of levels up the organizational chart.

Highly centralized organizations may not have knowledge of location-specific issues or problems. A decentralized supply chain can allow for faster issue resolution by individual locations and facilitate creative solutions.

Moreover, a platform that connects a company's different locations can help the organization coordinate decision-making and enable collaboration and transparency.

CHAPTER II

SUPPLY CHAIN INTEGRATES

Supply Chain Integrates- Push, Pull Strategies – Demand Driven Strategies – Impact on Grocery Industry – Retail Industry – Distribution Strategies.

An integrated supply chain can be defined as an association of customers and suppliers who, using management techniques, work together to optimize their collective performance in the creation, distribution, and support of an end product. If we move to a higher level, the next step would be to integrate the companies more closely. The circuit board supplier may construct a plant close to the assembly plant and may also share production software. Hence, the circuit board company would be able to see how many boards are required in the upcoming month and can construct them in time, as the company requires them in order to meet its sales demand.

This assures that the company has the appropriate materials required to produce the expected output of computers during the year. In the meanwhile, this computer company may sign a bond with a large supplier of circuit boards; the bond expects it to deliver a precise quantity at precise times within a year and fix a price that will be effective during the bond year. Further higher level is referred as vertical integration. This level starts when the supply chain of a company is actually owned by the company itself. Here, a computer company may buy the circuit board company just to ensure a devoted supply of elements.

MRS. POORNIMA G, ASSISTANT PROFESSOR IN COMMERCE, A J K COLLEGE OF ARTS AND SCIENCE COIMBATORE

Supply Chain Challenges with Data Management and Integration

At the core of all these supply chain challenges, from globalization to compliance, is the need for better data management and integration. Faced by global operations, market expansions, and stricter quality and regulatory standards, enterprises are getting overwhelmed by massive amounts of information coming from different suppliers and customers in varying geographic locations that they need to properly manage. This includes data from every stage of the supply chain such as pricing of direct and indirect materials, labour agreements, rental contracts, tax documents, freight bills, and compliance certificates, among many others. Data management and integration is key to solving these challenges by connecting the manufacturer's supply chain management systems with those of their suppliers and partners. Data management and integration give manufacturers much-needed visibility and control over all of their supply chain processes such as procurement, manufacturing, storage, and logistics.

Raw information coming from suppliers, partners, and even customers are also often composed of both structured and unstructured data which makes it even more difficult for enterprises to consume, analyse, and generate insights from these disjointed pieces of information. Proper data management and integration transform this raw information into compatible formats required by different supply chain management systems to ensure their seamless flow. Data management and integration address supply chain management challenges at the most basic level of the value chain and in every activity. Furthermore, providing visibility not only to manufacturers, but also to suppliers and partners can potentially improve trust and long- term relationships.

A Powerful Data Management and Integration Tool for Manufacturers:

Open Text's data solutions for the manufacturing industry enable manufacturers to overcome their supply chain challenges. They help enterprises globally manage and seamlessly integrate mission-critical data to improve efficiencies in forecasting, inventory management, material procurement, stock replenishment, order fulfillment, supply chain, and other key manufacturing processes.

Delivered using the Alloy Platform, Open Text's integration and data management solutions support the storage, integration, and syndication activities that enable manufacturers to grow a repository of quality data from their production process and supply chain. It also consolidates, cleanses, and enriches data coming from any number of disparate sources helping manufacturers keep up with globalization; respond to changing market needs, and meet quality and compliance requirements.

Push System:

A push-based supply chain is time consuming when it has to respond to fluctuations in demand, which can result in overstocking or bottlenecks and delays, unacceptable service levels and product obsolescence. A push system (also called make-to-stock) means that a company produces goods according to a demand forecast. It is often used to produce goods with a low chance of unforeseeable demand fluctuations, e.g. food, pharmaceuticals, household chemicals, etc.

This system is based on the deliberation of customer's demand. It tries to push as many products into the market as possible. As a result, the production is time consuming because the producer and the retailer struggle to react to the changes in the market. Forecast or prediction plays an important role in the push system. Optimum level of products can be produced through long term prediction. This deliberative nature of the push system leads to high production cost, high inventory cost as well as high shipment cost due to the company's desire to halt products at every stage.

Pull System

The pull-based supply chain is based on demand-driven techniques; the procurement, production and distribution are demand-driven rather than predicting. This system doesn't always follow the make-to-order production. For example, Toyota MotorsManufacturing produces products yet do not religiously produce to order. They follow the supermarket model.

According to this model, limited inventory is kept and piled up as it is consumed. Talking about Toyota, Kanban cards are used to hint at the requirement of piling up inventory. The major drawback in this system is that in case the demand exceeds than the amount of products manufactured, then the company fails to meet the customer demand, which in turn leads to loss of opportunity cost.

Basically in the pull system, the total time allotted for manufacturing of products is not sufficient. The production unit and distribution unit of the company rely on the demand. From this point of view, we can say that the company has a reactive supply chain.

Thus, it has less inventories as well as variability. It minimizes the lead time in the complete process. The biggest drawback in pull based supply chain integration is that it can't minimize the price by ranking up the production and operations.

A pull system is a lean manufacturing strategy used to reduce waste in the production process. In this type of system, components used in the manufacturing process are only replaced once they have been consumed so companies only make enough products to meet customer demand.

A great example of a pull system is just-in-time manufacturing. The core idea of JIT is to schedule the process so that materials would reach the facility exactly when production is scheduled to start, and production is scheduled so that it would be finished just as the goods should be dispatched to the customer.

Differences in Push and Pull System

The major differences between push and pull view in supply chain are as follows:

- In the push system, the implementation begins in anticipation of customer order whereas in the pull system, the implementation starts as a result of customer's order
- In the push system, there is an uncertainty in demand whereas in pull system, the demand remains certain
- The push system is a speculative process whereas the pull system is a reactive process.
- The level of complexity is high in the push system whereas it is low in the pull system.
- The push based system concentrates on resources allocation whereas the pull system stresses on responsiveness.
- The push system has a long lead time whereas the pull system has a short lead time.

Push & Pull System

Mostly we find a supply chain as merger of both push and pull systems, where the medium between the stages of the push-based and the pull-based systems is referred as the push–pull boundary.

The terms push and pull were framed in logistics and supply chain management, but these terms are broadly used in the field of marketing as well as in the hotel distribution business.

To present an example, Wal-Mart implements the push vs. pull strategy. A push and pull system in business represents the shipment of a product or information between two subjects. Generally, the consumers use pull system in the markets for the goods or information they demand for their requirements whereas the merchants or suppliers use the push system towards the consumers.

In supply chains, all the levels or stages function actively for the push and the pull system. The production in push system depends on the demand predicted and production in pull system depends on absolute or consumed demand.

The medium between these two levels is referred as the push–pull boundary or decoupling point. Generally, this strategy is recommended for products where uncertainty in demand is high. Further, economies of scale play a crucial role in minimizing production and/or delivery costs.

For example, the furniture industries use the push and pull strategy. Here the production unit uses the pull-based strategy because it is impossible to make production decisions on the basis on long term prediction. Meanwhile, the distribution unit needs to enjoy the benefits of economy of scale so that the shipment cost can be reduced; thus it uses a push-based strategy.

Process View of Supply Chain and Supply Chain Models

The process view of the supply chain indicates that the supply chain is a sequence of processes that connect the members of the supply chain through the flow of material, information, and funds.

The process view of the supply chain can be explained under two headings:

1. Cycle view
2. Push and pull view

Cycle View of Supply Chain

The cycle view of the supply chain indicates that the supply chain is a series of processes performed at the interface of any two stages of the supply chain. This can be understood with an example.

The supply chain of a manufacturer who manufactures and sells the products through the distributor and the retailer will undergo four major supply chain processes namely Purchase the raw material, Manufacture the product., Distribute and stock the products with the distributors and Deliver the products as the customer orders through the retailer.

The supply chain process, when viewed as a cycle is as follows:

- The process at the interface between the Supplier and manufacturer is the procurement cycle
- The process at the next interface between the manufacturer and distributor is the Manufacturing cycle

- The process at the next link between the distributor and retailer is stock replenishment cycle
- The process at the next interface between the retailer and the customer is customer order fulfillment cycle.

The process view of supply chain indicates that

1. Not all supply chains have to move through all the interfaces, some supply chains will not have one or more interfaces.

For example, a retailer who does not manufacture the products but only sells will not have the manufacturing cycle and a manufacturer who distributes the products through its retail outlets will have a stock replenishment cycle at the interface between the manufacturer and the retailer. Each cycle consists of various sub-processes. The sub-processes are triggered by the orders placed by the customers or when the demand for the product is anticipated and then the products are produced and end when the product is delivered and services rendered to the customers.

These sub processes across the cycle are the same as in the SCOR model processes of the plan, source, make, deliver, and return. The supply chain operational decisions are based on the process view of the supply chain and the responsiveness of the supply chain.

The next category in the process view of the supply chain is Push and pulls view of supply chain

Push and Pull View of Supply Chain

The process view supply chain is defined as pull or push. The push and pull view of a supply chain focuses on the supply chain responsiveness. The supply chains can respond to the anticipatory demand of the customer (push processes) or after the actual demand from the customer (pull processes).

Supply Chain Responsiveness

Supply chain responsiveness is the ability of the supply chain to cater to the huge quantities demanded, respond to the assortments and variety of products demanded by the customers, deliver the products within a short time after the customer has initiated his demand, manage high-quality service levels, ensure that uncertainties in supply does not affect the product delivery and initiate and support innovative product design and delivery.

The responsiveness of the supply chain can be triggered at two points

- On anticipation of the future demand of the customer or
- In response to customer order

The supply chain processes in anticipation of the customer order are push processes and the supply chain processes in response to the customer order are pulled processes.

Push and Pull Supply Chain

Push and pull strategies evolved as a marketing concept and it can be understood as follows:

You are having a grocery list of items to purchase. At the supermarket (A), you don't find the items you required. So, you move to the other supermarket (B), where you find the required items. Here Supermarket (B) has anticipated your monthly demand and stocked the products and brands in required assortments to attract you and pushed you towards their store. This is Push Strategy. Likewise, supermarket (B) had also made some attractive display of some products near the cash counters. And even though those items are not in your list. You get attracted and buy a product. This is a Pull strategy.

A supply chain is an integral part of marketing and customer satisfaction and hence supply chains are designed to meet the push and pull marketing strategies.

Push Supply Chain (Anticipatory Business Model)

The push supply chain is also known as an anticipatory business model. In a push supply chain strategy, the supply chain function is to supply products that are manufactured and stocked based on the long-term demand forecast. Each partner in the supply chain holds inventory to meet the anticipatory demand. It is based on the make-to-stock policy.

Push supply chains are adopted when firms follow the anticipatory business model, purchase behavior is not certain due to lack of real-time market information, firms are involved in mass production and have high volume scales and huge market share, manufacturers produce products based on demand forecast and not after receiving the order, firms plan to meet existing demand within short lead time and firms want to avoid stock-outs.

The challenges when following a push supply chain strategy are:

- Forecast not being accurate can lead to differences in what the firm planned to do and what the firm did.
- Uncertainty and unplanned inventory.
- Inability to meet sudden hike in demand for products or changing demands.

- Conflict of interest among the trading partners.
- Risk of product obsolescence

Procure Make Stock Sell Deliver Demand

Forecast In the traditional push strategy, the flow of information, products, and negotiations is unidirectional that is from manufacturers to the customers.

An example of a push supply chain strategy is that of a retail outlet who anticipate the seasonal demand changes in readymade garments and accessories. Even before the summer season the apparel brands design the summer collections and promote their designs. Another example is the mobile brands that follow an anticipatory business model and their supply chain logistics are driven by demand forecast and inventory management.

Pull strategy is followed by firms that adopt a responsive business model that is made to order philosophy. The logistics of the supply chain is based on the real-time information of the point of sale data and is driven by actual customer demand.

The pull supply chain is triggered when the customer order is received. This supply chain strategy has the advantage of less wastage in case of low demand.

The pull supply chain is practiced when manufacturer follows build to order business, the scope of customization to meet customer demand is high, the supply chain is demand-driven, customer involvement and knowledge demands direct connectivity, firms aim at reducing inventory level and inventory carrying cost, and flexibility to change customer services to change in demand is mandatory.

The challenges are inventory shortage to meet rising demands, flexibility in manufacturing and distribution demands agile supply chains, customization of manufacturing and delivery involves operational risk of multiple channel partner management, obtaining and sharing accurate sales data from all supply chain partners is risky and high cost and risk of shortening the lead time.

An example of a pull supply chain process is a fashion designer who produces apparel for customers after receiving the order and its specification from the customers is an example of a pull supply chain. Other examples are computer brands that assemble computers after receiving customer orders, Designer automobile suppliers, and Automobile service centers.

Push, Pull and Postponement Supply Chain Strategy

With the industrial and information technology revolution, time-based competition is prevailing in all businesses and this has led to the blending of push and pull supply chain strategy.

In supply chain management terms, the blending of push and pull supply chains is termed as Push/pull boundary.

Push and Pull Boundary

Business firms today do not follow pure pull strategy or pure push strategy instead they have few supply chain processes based on anticipatory demand and the others based on actual demand. The firms set boundaries as to which of the supply chain processes should be push processes and which of them should be pull processes.

CUSTOMER ORDER ARRIVES

This process classification as pull processes and push processes sets the push/pull boundary. The interface between the push-based stages and the pull-based stages is the push-pull boundary

For example, if an apparel manufacturer makes 100 sweaters of standard size and stocks them but dyes the sweaters based on real-time order and delivers them as ordered his supply chain and the push-pull boundary is at dyeing the sweaters Thus, in practice, the supply chain process involves:

- Identifying supply chain processes that depend on anticipatory demand and the others that can focus on actual demand and
- Defining the push and pull boundary that can match supply and demand effectively.

With the advent of information technology, the supply chain is designed as Pull based push strategy wherein the information flow to the customer can be directly from the manufacturer or through the supply chain partners; the product flow is from the manufacturer through the supply chain partners. And the negotiation flow is bi-directional between the customer and the manufacturer either directly or through channel partners.

The other examples of the push-pull boundary are:

1. A computer manufacturer produces the various components of a computer and holds stock of them but assembles and delivers the computer only on receiving the customer order. The push- pull boundary is at the

stage between Procurement cycle and Manufacturing cycle

2. A paint manufacturer produces various standard colors of paints and stocks them at retail outlets but mixes the paint and delivers them as per the customer choice.

The push and pull boundary is between the Retailer and customer stage that is between the replenishment cycle and customer order cycle.

1. Boutiques holds various apparel materials in stock but does designing, stitching, and deliver on scheduled time after receiving the order from the customer. The push and pull boundary is between the procurement cycle and the manufacturing cycle.

The blending of push-pull strategy as a pull based push strategy has led to a supply chain strategy called postponement.

Postponement Strategy

Postponement strategy is producing and holding inventory of a standard product state based on anticipated demand but postponing the final manufacturing, customization, or distribution of the product until the customer order is received. *The two types of postponement are:*

1. Manufacturing postponement
2. Geographical postponement

Manufacturing Postponement:

Manufacturing or form postponement involves manufacturing a standard or a base product in sufficient quantities while holding back the finalization of the customized features until the customer places the order.

For example, a car manufacturer manufactures the standard car but postpones the customization of features like car colour, seats audio system, etc. until the customer places the order for a car.

Geographic Postponement:

In geographic postponement, the products are manufactured and stocked in one strategic location but the delivery of inventory is postponed until the customer order is received.

A retail chain that sells its brands across the world can anticipate the seasonal demand and produce the apparels and stock it in the central warehouse which is strategically located. It captures the point of sale data from various retail outlets and then decides which assortment in what quantity should be deployed to each region. This is geographic postponement.

Exercise: Visit any firm and map the supply chain processes and define their push, pull, and postponement strategies.

Demand-Driven Strategies

The demand-driven strategies were first developed to understand the impact of inactivity and collection, as information fertilizes the supply chain from the source of demand to the suppliers.

Within a mentioned supply lead time, normally the manufacturers manufacture sufficient goods to satisfy the needs of their clients predicted. But this is only somewhat accurate at the granular level at which inventory decisions are made.

Anyways, when the actual demand varies from the demand predicted, the first thing to be done is to adjust the supply levels needed in accordance with each step of the supply chain. But because of time delay between changing demands and its detection at several at points along the supply chain, its impact is amplified, resulting in inventory shortages or excesses.

The inventory levels of the companies are disturbed because of the overcompensation done by the companies either by slowing down or speeding up production. These fluctuations prove to be a costly and inefficient affair for all participants.

Basically, the demand-driven strategies or the demand-driven supply chain is completely based on the demand as well as the supply part of marketing. So it can be uniquely organized in terms of the demand side and supply side initiatives.

The demand-side initiatives concentrate on efficient methods to acquire the demand signal closer to the source, observe the demand to sense the latest and most accurate demand signal and shape the demand by implementing and following promotional and pricing strategies to gear up demand in accordance with business objectives.

ROLE OF IT

On the other hand, the supply side initiatives mostly need to do with reducing reliance on the prediction by developing into an agile supply chain accompanied by faster response when absolute demand is known.

All the strategies discussed above are addressed under the demand-driven strategy, but we a company following all of them is rare. In fact, we can conclude that companies concentrate on different markets on the basis of features of the market and industry.

Companies that opt to participate in supply chain management initiatives accept a specific role to enact. They have a mutual feeling that they, along with all other supply chain participants, will be better off because of this collaborative effort. The fundamental issue here is power. The last two decades have seen the shifting of power from manufacturers to retailers.

When we talk about information access for the supply chain, retailers have an essential designation. They emerge to the position of prominence with the help of technologies. The Advancement of inter-organizational information system for the supply chain has three distinct benefits. These are:

Cost Reduction: The advancement of technology has further led to ready availability of all the products with different offers and discounts. This leads to reduction of costs of products.

Productivity: The growth of information technology has improved productivity because of inventions of new tools and software. That makes productivity much easier and less time consuming.

Improvement and Product/Market Strategies: Recent years have seen a huge growth in not only the technologies but the market itself. New strategies are made to allure customers and new ideas are being experimented for improving the product.

It would be appropriate to say that information technology is a vital organ of supply chain management.

With the advancement of technologies, new products are being introduced within a fraction of second increasing their demand in the market. Let us study the role of information technology in supply chain management briefly.

The software as well as the hardware part needs to be considered in the advancement and maintenance of supply chain information systems. The hardware part comprises the computer's input/output devices like the screen, printer, mouse, and storage media. The software part comprises the entire system and application program used for processing transactions management control, decision-making, and strategic planning. Here we will be discussing the role of some critical hardware and software devices in SCM. These are briefed below:

ELECTRONIC COMMERCE

Electronic commerce involves a broad range of tools and techniques used to conduct business in a paperless environment. Hence it comprises electronic data interchange, email, electronic fund transfers, electronic publishing, image processing, electronic bulletin boards, shared databases and magnetic/optical data capture. Electronic commerce helps enterprises to automate the process of transferring records, documents, data and information electronically between suppliers and customers, thus making the communication process a lot easier, cheaper and less time consuming.

Types of E-Commerce Models

Electronic commerce can be classified into four main categories. The basis for this simple classification is the parties that are involved in the transactions. *So the four basic electronic commerce models are as follows,*

Business to Business: This is Business to Business transactions. Here the companies are doing business with each other. The final consumer is not involved. So the online transactions only involve the manufacturers, wholesalers, retailers etc.

Business to Consumer: Business to Consumer. Here the company will sell their goods and/or services directly to the consumer. The consumer can browse their websites and look at products, pictures, read reviews. Then they place their order and the company ships the goods directly to them. Popular examples are Amazon, Flipkart, and Jabong etc.

Consumer to Consumer: Consumer to consumer, where the consumers are in direct contact with each other. No company is involved. It helps people sell their personal goods and assets directly to an interested party. Usually, goods traded are cars, bikes, electronics etc. OLX, Quikr etc. follow this model.

Consumer to Business: This is the reverse of B2C; it is a consumer to business. So the consumer provides a good or some service to the company. Say for example an IT freelancer who demos and sells his software to a company. This would be a C2B transaction.

Advantages of E-Commerce

- E-commerce provides the sellers with a global reach. They remove the barrier of place (geography). Now sellers and buyers can meet in the virtual world, without the hindrance of location.

- Electronic commerce will substantially lower the transaction cost. It eliminates many fixed costs of maintaining brick and mortar shops. This allows the companies to enjoy a much higher margin of profit.
- It provides quick delivery of goods with very little effort on part of the customer. Customer complaints are also addressed quickly. It also saves time, energy and effort for both the consumers and the company.
- One other great advantage is the convenience it offers. A customer can shop 24×7. The website is functional at all times; it does not have working hours like a shop.
- Electronic commerce also allows the customer and the business to be in touch directly, without any intermediaries. This allows for quick communication and transactions. It also gives a valuable personal touch.

Disadvantages of E-Commerce

- The start-up costs of the e-commerce portal are very high. The setup of the hardware and the software, the training cost of employees, the constant maintenance and upkeep are all quite expensive.
- Although it may seem like a sure thing, the e-commerce industry has a high risk of failure. Many companies riding the dot-com wave of the 2000s have failed miserably. The high risk of failure remains even today.
- At times, e-commerce can feel impersonal. So it lacks the warmth of an interpersonal relationship which is important for many brands and products. This lack of

a personal touch can be a disadvantage for many types of services and products like interior designing or the jewelry business.

- Security is another area of concern. Only recently, we have witnessed many security breaches where the information of the customers was stolen. Credit card theft, identity theft etc. remain big concerns with the customers.
- Then there are also fulfillment problems. Even after the order is placed there can be problems with shipping, delivery, mix-ups etc. This leaves the customers unhappy and dissatisfied.

Benefits of e-commerce:

1. **Convenience:** Online commerce makes purchases simpler, faster, and less time-consuming, allowing for 24-hour sales, quick delivery, and easy returns.
2. **Personalization and Customer Experience:** E-commerce marketplaces can create rich user profiles that allow them to personalize the products offered and make suggestions for other products that they might find interesting. This improves the customer experience by making shoppers feel understood on a personal level, increasing the odds of brand loyalty.
3. **Global Marketplace:** Customers from around the world can easily shop e-commerce sites – companies are no longer restricted by geography or physical barriers.
4. **Minimized Expenses:** Since brick and mortar is no longer required, digital sellers can launch online stores with minimal startup and operating costs.

5. **Convenience:** Online commerce makes purchases simpler, faster, and less time-consuming, allowing for 24-hour sales, quick delivery, and easy returns.

6. **Personalization and Customer Experience:** E-commerce marketplaces can create rich user profiles that allow them to personalize the products offered and make suggestions for other products that they might find interesting. This improves the customer experience by making shoppers feel understood on a personal level, increasing the odds of brand loyalty.

7. **Global Marketplace:** Customers from around the world can easily shop e-commerce sites – companies are no longer restricted by geography or physical barriers.

8. **Minimized Expenses:** Since brick and mortar is no longer required, digital sellers can launch online stores with minimal startup and operating costs.

9. **Convenience:** Online commerce makes purchases simpler, faster, and less time-consuming, allowing for 24-hour sales, quick delivery, and easy returns.

10. **Personalization and Customer Experience:** E-commerce marketplaces can create rich user profiles that allow them to personalize the products offered and make suggestions for other products that they might find interesting. This improves the customer experience by making shoppers feel understood on a personal level, increasing the odds of brand loyalty.

11. **Global Marketplace:** Customers from around the world can easily shop e-commerce sites – companies are no longer restricted by geography or physical barriers.

12. **Minimized Expenses:** Since brick and mortar is no longer required, digital sellers can launch online stores with minimal startup and operating costs.

ELECTRONIC DATA INTERCHANGE

Electronic Data Interchange (EDI) involves the swapping of business documents in a standard format from computer-to-computer. It presents the capability as well as the practice of exchanging information between two companies electronically rather than the traditional form of mail, courier, & fax.

The major advantages of EDI are as follows:

- Instant processing of information
- Improvised customer service
- Limited paper work
- High productivity
- Advanced tracing and expediting
- Cost efficiency
- Competitive benefit
- Advanced billing

The application of EDI supply chain partners can overcome the deformity and falsehood in supply and demand information by remodeling technologies to support real time sharing of actual demand and supply information.

Key Benefits of the Electronic Data Interchange

Reduced Costs:

- EDI transactions reduce expenses related to paper, printing, copy, storage, filing, postage and document retrieval. In addition, EDI lowers the dealings prices by a minimum of 35%

- A major electronics manufacturer calculates the value of process an order manually at $38 compared to only $1.35 for an order processed mistreatment EDI
- EDI saves employees valuable time by reducing errors caused due to unreadable faxes, lost orders or incorrectly taken phone orders.

Enhanced Speed and Accuracy:

- EDI speeds up your business cycles by 61%. Exchange transactions in minutes rather than the times or weeks of wait time from the postal service
- EDI improves data quality, delivering a minimum of a 30–40% reduction in transactions with errors — climinating crrors from markcd-up handwriting, lost faxes/mail and keying, and re-keying errors.
- Using EDI will scale back the order-to-cash cycle time by quite the 200th, rising business partner transactions and relationships.

Increased Efficiency:

- Automating paper-based tasks enables business executives to invest more time in higher-value tasks
- Faster processing of business documents results in less re-working of orders, fewer stock-outs and reduced off orders.
- Automating the exchange information between applications ensures that business-critical data is distributed on time

- Shortening the order process and delivery times means organizations will cut back their inventory levels.

Improved Business Strategies

- Enables period of time visibility into transaction status. This successively allows quicker decision-making and improved responsiveness to dynamic client and market demands and permits businesses to adopt a demand-driven business model instead of a supply-driven one.
- EDI reduces the lead times for product enhancements and new product delivery.
- Streamlines your ability to enter new territories and markets. EDI provides a standard business language that facilitates business partner onboarding anyplace within the world.
- Promotes company social responsibility and sustainability by substitution paper-based processes with electronic alternatives. this may each prevent cash and cut back your co2 emissions.

Technical Architecture of the Electronic Data Interchange

In Electronic Data Interchange (EDI), three types of protocols are used for receiving and sending files from one place to another.

File Transfer Protocol (FTP):

FTP is a robust, reliable file transfer protocol developed and utilized by several businesses significantly for file exchange inside a corporation. However, FTP alone doesn't give the protection required for document exchange with different corporations over the web. For this reason, businesses that use FTP use it in conjunction with VPN computer code, which provides the required protection layer.

Value-Added Network (VAN):

VAN is a non-public network provider whereby EDI (Electronic Data Interchange) documents are transmitted and exchanged. In alternative words, it's a channel of communication to move data from point A to point B.

AS2:

AS2 is one of the most popular ways of transporting data, particularly EDI data, securely and reliably over the web. It basically involves 2 computers — a client and a server — connecting in a very point-to-point manner via the web. AS2 creates an "envelope" for the EDI data, permitting it to be sent securely — using digital certificates and encryption — over the web.

Barcode Scanning:

We can see the application of barcode scanners in the checkout counters of super market. This code states the name ofthe product along with its manufacturer. Some other practical applications of barcode scanners are tracking the moving items like elements in PC assembly operations and automobiles in assembly plants.

Data Warehouse:

Data warehouse can be defined as a store comprising all the databases. It is a centralized database that is prolonged independently from the production system database of a company. Many companies maintain multiple databases. Instead of some particular business processes, it is established around informational subjects. The data present in data warehouses is time dependent and easily accessible. Historical data may also be accumulated in data warehouse.

Enterprise Resource Planning (ERP) Tools

The ERP system has now become the base of many IT infrastructures. Some of the ERP tools are Baan, SAP, and People Soft. ERP system has now become the processing tool of many companies. They grab the data and minimize the manual activities and tasks related to processing financial, inventory and customer order information.

ERP system holds a high level of integration that is achieved through the proper application of a single data model, improving mutual understanding of what the shared data represents and constructing a set of rules for accessing data.

With the advancement of technology, we can say that world is shrinking day by day. Similarly, customers' expectations are increasing. Also companies are being more prone to uncertain environment. In this running market, a company can only sustain if it accepts the fact that their conventional supply chain integration needs to be expanded beyond their peripheries.

The strategic and technological interventions in supply chain have a huge effect in predicting the buy and sell features of a company. A company should try to use the potential of the internet to the maximum level through clear vision, strong planning and technical insight. This is essential for better supply chain management and also for improved competitiveness.

We can see how Internet technology, World Wide Web, electronic commerce etc. has changed the way in which a company does business. These companies must acknowledge the power of technology to work together with their business partners.

We can in fact say that IT has launched a new breed of SCM application. The Internet and other networking links learn from the performance in the past and observe the historical trends in order to identify how much product should be made along with the best and cost effective methods for warehousing it or shipping it to retailer.

SCM- AGILE AND REVERSE SUPPLY CHAINS

In this chapter, we will throw some light on two specialized supply chains — Agile Supply Chain Reverse
Supply Chain

Agile Supply Chain:
An agile supply chain can be defined as a chain of supply that has the potential to respond to changing requirements in a way that accelerates the delivery of ordered goods to customers.

In simple words, supply chain agility is a custom adopted by many companies for choosing a dealer. As we know, a supply chain with flexibility and the ability to quickly react to emergency requirements can help the business answer more efficiently to its customers. Apart from flexibility, speed and accuracy are also signature marks of this type of supply chain.

To acknowledge the advantages of an agile supply chain, we have to learn about the elements of any type of supply chain. These include elements like collection of orders and processing, supply of materials to create the goods used to complete orders, packaging and transport of finished goods, and the quality of customer service that is advertised throughout the process from the point of sale to the actual delivery and beyond.

Thus, for considering the functions of supply chain as agile, each one of these elements must be managed efficiently and coordinated in such a way that makes it possible to adapt to changing circumstances.

With the help of an agile supply chain, merchants can easily respond to the varying requirements of customer with relatively less time required. For example, if a client has already placed a sizable order but demands the product to be delivered few days prior to the projected delivery date, a merchant with a truly agile supply chain can easily accommodate that change in the client's situation, at least in part. Working collaboratively, the merchant and the customer develop a strategy to permit the delivery of as much of the order as possible within the new time frame required.

There are times when merchants need to think creatively along with some flexibility in terms of scheduling production time, selecting shippers and basically looking closely at each step in the order completion process to search for ways to reduce the time required to successfully accomplish those tasks and abide with the customer's request.

Reverse Supply Chain:

Reverse supply chain states the evolution of products from customer to merchant. This is the reverse of the traditional supply chain evolution of products from merchant to customer.

Reverse logistics is the process of planning, executing, monitoring and controlling the efficient and effective inbound flow and storage of secondary goods and information related to the purpose of recovering value or proper disposal. Some examples of reverse supply chain are as follows:

- Product returns and handling product displacement.
- Remanufacturing and refurbishing exercises.
- Management and sale of surplus, along with returned equipment and machines from the hardware leasing business.

Different types of reverse supply chain arise at different stages of the product cycle. *Mostly reverse supply chain is designed to carry out the below given five key processes:*

Product Acquisition: Accumulating the used product from the user by the reseller or manufacturer because of some manufacturing defect or some other reason. It is basically considered as a company's growth strategy.

Reverse Logistics: Shipping of products from their final destination for auditing, sorting and disposition.

Inspection and Disposition: Examining the condition of the product returned along with making the most profitable decision for reusing it in some other way.

Remanufacturing or Refurnishing: Returning the product to its original source from where it was ordered in the very first place along with specifications. This is done basically when there is a manufacturing or furnishing defect in the goods.

Marketing: Establishing secondary markets for the goods that have been recovered by the merchant from the client who initially ordered it in the beginning but chose to return it.

In short, we can say that the enterprises that closely coordinate with their forward supply chains are the one that have been most successful with their reverse supply chains. These two chains create a closed-loop system. For example, the company designs a product layout according to the manufacturing decisions followed by recycling and reconditioning. Bosch is a beautiful example of reverse supply chain. It constructs sensors into the motors of its power tools, which signs if the motor is worth reconditioning.

Technology plays a great role here by reducing the inspection and disposition costs, sanctioning the company to make a profit on the remanufactured tools. In fact, along with reverse supply chains, forward thinking results in big dividends.

Impact on Grocery Industry

Groceries are sold by many other stores, such as convenience stores, drug stores, and dollar stores. The result of retail channel blurring is that even when people are buying groceries, only about half of them are buying groceries from a grocery store. Online sales of food are small but increasing.

Grocery Supply Chain Work:

To help ensure consistency and ease of operations, supermarkets leverage wholesale grocers to aid them in merchandise distribution. While wholesale grocers bridge the gap between product manufacturers, food producers and retailers, they also may sell goods to other wholesalers or distribution companies.

Grocery Retail Strategies Fall Flat If Not Backed by the Right Supply Chains:

Food retail is a tough and turbulent market. Grocery has never been easy, but the current business transformation is more dramatic than anything we have seen in decades, especially with COVID-19 further accelerating many trends shaping the market. Grocery retailers need to simultaneously address several major trends:

Breakneck Developments in Online Ordering and Order Fulfillment Options:

From online ordering to home delivery and curb side pickup, the speed of Omni channel development has made operational efficiency particularly challenging for food retailers due to their mix of low- value products and high handling costs for fragile, variously sized products that often require temperature control. But while many struggle to make e-grocery profitable, few food retailers can afford not to go online.

Discounters have Demonstrated the Power of Operational Efficiency:

Since 2008's financial crisis, discounters have grown their market share, proving that shoppers appreciate low-cost private label products and well-curated assortments, even at the expense of abundant choice. Cost control always provides a competitive advantage, especially when consumers are hesitant to spend, so streamlining operations to improve efficiency must be a key part of every grocery retailer's strategy going forward.

Grocery Retailers must also Compete with the Food Service Industry:

Restaurants, meal delivery services, and food-to-go are capturing an increasing share of consumers' wallets. As a result, food retailers are turning to prepared meals to increase relevance and high-value food-to-go items to improve margins in a tough environment. Some are even opening in-store restaurants. With poor execution, though, these initiatives also introduce new opportunities to lose money on costly food waste.

Spotlight on Challenging Fresh and Short Shelf Life Products:

Healthy eating trends have even discounters like Aldi and Lidl improving their fresh offerings to include organic meats and freshly baked breads. In their pursuit of growth, these former hard discounters are stepping away from their highly efficient comfort zones previously built on simplicity, standardization, and large volumes. The increasing complexity as they experiment with fresher products, smaller store formats, and localized assortments will put their grocery supply chains to the test.

The Push Toward Sustainability:

Consumers' environmental concerns are only growing, and they expect their grocers to develop sustainable practices too. Many leading retailers have already committed to lowering their carbon emissions, but very soon, sustainability will move from "positive messaging" to table stakes. Retailers who fail to take meaningful action to reduce waste and emissions put their reputations at risk. The good news is that sustainability, efficiency, and profitability, in many cases, go hand in hand.

Harness the Power of AI to Optimize Your Grocery Supply Chain:

Today's grocers collect massive amounts of data on transactions and interactions with consumers both on- and offline. That's precisely why grocery retail is the perfect match for artificial intelligence (AI), which makes it possible to leverage that data into faster, more accurate decisions. This is an invaluable asset in an industry where retailers must control millions of goods. Flows and accurately match supply to demand at hundreds or even thousands of locations on a daily basis.

Technology companies can be eager to position their AI algorithms as "intelligent" by making them as human as possible even giving them human names like Siri, Alexa, Einstein, or Watson. Keep in mind, though, that AI is not a person. AI is not even a singular "it."

We are still far from general artificial intelligence that would be able to creatively solve ill-defined problems. We are, however, making great progress in specialized AI that solves well- defined problems (such as algorithms for image recognition) and combinations of several types of Specialized AI (such as self-driving cars).

Demand Forecasting is the Engine Running Your Grocery Supply Chain Demand forecasting is the engine running your grocery supply chain. Yet, despite the technology available, a great number of notable grocery retailers have yet to truly embark on their journey of data-driven forecasting.

Granular, Data-Driven Forecasting Is A Must for Grocery Retailers: Granular forecasting is not just a best practice—it's a must-have in today's grocery retail. Without detailed forecasts, it's impossible to correctly position inventory in the supply chain to maximize sales and minimize waste. Granular forecasts are also the planning foundation for both resource and capacity management, and thus should be considered a prerequisite for profitable operations.

Machine Learning Delivers High Value in Grocery Demand Forecasting: What started with a few forerunners like RELEX has become mainstream over the years: <u>machine learning for retail demand forecasting</u>. Currently, retail technology vendors either apply machine learning or are rushing to update their legacy systems to offer it. Machine learning gives a forecasting system the ability to learn automatically and improve its predictions using data alone, with no additional programming needed. Because retailers generate enormous amounts of data, machine learning technology quickly proves its value.

Typical Demand Forecasting Challenges for Supermarkets, Discounters, and Convenience Stores: Next, we will discuss how you can overcome some of the typical forecasting challenges that supermarkets, discounters, and convenience stores face.

Predicting Demand for New Products and Stores: Because machine learning relies on finding patterns in historical sales data, new products with no historical sales data can prove a challenge. Fortunately, further routines are available to improve the management of new product introductions as well. When introducing a new product, the most common approach is to assign it a reference product to use as a blueprint for its sales pattern until the new product has accumulated sufficient historical data of its own. However, in grocery retail, the number of new products per year can be massive. This makes manually identifying and setting reference products infeasible, or at least highly inefficient.

Forecasting the Impact of Promotions and Price & Display Changes

Your own business decisions as a retailer are also an important source of demand variation, from promotions and price changes to adjustments in how products are displayed throughout your stores. Despite the fact that retailers plan and control these changes themselves, many in the industry remain incapable of accurately predicting their impact.

A product's pricing in relation to other products in its category often has a large impact as well. In many categories, the product with the lowest price captures a disproportionally large share of demand. Machine learning-based demand forecasting makes it quite straightforward to consider a product's price position.

Machine learning does more than simply leverage price data, though. With machine learning forecasting, grocery retailers can accurately predict the impact of promotions by taking into consideration factors including, but by no means limited to:

- Promotion type, such as price reduction or multi-buy
- Marketing activities, such as circular ads or in-store signage
- Products' price reductions
- In-store display, such as presenting the promoted product in an end cap or on a table.

Retail Industry:

By "retail" we mean the market that includes all those activities that involve the sale of goods or services by a company directly to the consumer that are usually purchased for personal or family use Retailers can be both retail and institutional.

Retail is the sale of goods and services to consumers, in contrast to wholesaling, which is sale to business or institutional customers. A retailer purchases goods in large quantities from manufacturers, directly or through a wholesaler, and then sells in smaller quantities to consumers for a profit.

Retail Supply Chain Management is the process of managing the entire supply chain of retail organizations. The differentiating factor of retail supply chain management from other supply chain management is in the volume of product movement and the fast moving nature of the products of the retail industry.

DISTRIBUTION STRATEGY

Distribution strategy is the method used to bring products, goods and services to customers or end-users. You often gain repeat customers by ensuring an easy and effective way to get your goods and services to people, depending on the item and its distribution needs.

What is Distribution Strategy?

Distribution Strategy is a strategy or a plan to make a product or a service available to the target customers through its supply chain. Distribution strategy designs the entire approach for availability of the offering starting taking inputs from what the company communicated in marketing campaigns to what target audience is to be served. A company can decide whether it wants to serve the product and service through their own channels or partner with other companies to use their distribution channels to do the same.

Some companies can use their own exclusive stores for their own products or can use available retail chains to sell their products. It can be combination of both. Many companies these days also use online exclusive channels to sell their products or services.

Importance of Distribution Strategy

Distribution Strategy is precisely the strategy deployed by a company to make sure the product/service can reach the maximum potential customers at minimal or optimal distribution costs.

A good distribution strategy can maximize your revenue and profits but a bad and unplanned distribution strategy can lead not only to losses but also helping the competitors get the advantage through the opportunity in the market which you created.

Types of Distribution Strategy

Overall there are 3 major distribution strategies

Exclusive Distribution:

Exclusive stories to sell products leads to more control. This can be good for niche, luxury or specialty goods. **Example**, Luis Vuitton Stores

Intensive Distribution:

Maximizing outlets to maximize sales. This is good for mass products which have to reach maximum target audience and the manufacturing is also high as compared to other normal goods. **Example**, Coca Cola

Selective Distribution:

This approach includes carefully choosing multiple channels and partners. This is more hybrid approach and needs to be carefully formulated to make sure that there is optimized distribution of the product/service. **Example**, Adidas, Nike

These 3 distribution strategies are the most used but a typical strategy may differ for a particular product or a company. Many companies use online as well as offline strategies together to optimize sales e.g. Apple iPhone. In many situations one or more distribution channels can be used, for example (there are many more forms apart from these)

1. Manufacturer -> end customer
2. Manufacture -> agent -> end customer
3. Manufacturer -> retailer -> end customer
4. Manufacturer -> wholesaler -> retailer -> end customer
5. Manufacturer -> reseller -> retailer -> end customer
6. Manufacturer -> franchisor -> franchisee -> end customer

Distribution strategy should be optimized and updated regularly as per the market parameters through demand analysis and supply analysis so that it can keep up with the current market scenarios and does what it is intended to do i.e. make product reach to potential customers. Push or pull marketing strategies would both not work if a company's distribution strategy is not in place.

Factors affecting Distribution Strategy

Distribution Strategy depends upon following parameters too:

Location of Business:

This is one of the most important factors in deciding the distribution strategy. If location is business is at a place where distribution can be readily done like near a port or railway lines, then we can rely on that mode for distribution and save costs as well.

Location of Target Market:

Now distribution is done from manufacturer/ distributor/retailer to the end customer. If end customer is located or interacting with similar products at a particular location, then the distribution strategy needs to include it. If the target market is professionals, then the product should be available near offices or inside offices through partnerships so that the product is available where the demand is.

Reaching the Target Market:

The end goal of a product is to reach the target audience when required. Distribution strategy has to ensure that the product reaches the potential customers when they look for the same. During summers e.g. a beverage company would make sure that it is present in all retail stores in sufficient quantity.

Warehousing:

Properly storing the inventory at apt locations is an important aspect while deciding the distribution strategy. Warehousing and inventory management come into picture.

Transportation and Logistics:

Transportation is one of the most important aspect of distribution strategy. Without proper transportation either the product will not reach the target market in time or may be it would not be in right quality. e.g. if a company deals in frozen foods, then it needs to make sure that the transportation and logistics are taking care of that through cold storage and temperature maintenance.

Distribution Strategy Example

Let us take **example** of a soft drink manufacturer which glass bottles of the product. For a company to succeed, it needs to make sure that it is located at a place where the water is readily available and after manufacturing the bottles can be quickly filled and transported to the next channel. The glass bottles can be fragile so they need to make sure that the transportation is through robust packaging and storage. Same applies to the warehousing.

The other aspect is the distributional channel selection. Is the product going to be available to all retailers or is there a partnership with an exclusive partner to do the same? The distribution strategy has to make sure about intensive or exclusive strategy.

CHAPTER III

Strategic Alliances

Strategic Alliances: Frame Work for Strategic Alliances – 3PL – Merits and Demerits – Retailer – Supplier Partnership – Advantages and Disadvantages of RSP – Distributor Integration

A strategic alliance is an arrangement between two companies to undertake a mutually beneficial project while each retains its independence. The agreement is less complex and less binding than a joint venture, in which two businesses pool resources to create a separate business entity. Further higher level is referred as vertical integration. This level starts when the supply chain of a company is actually owned by the company itself. Here, a computer company may buy the circuit board company just to ensure a devoted supply of elements.

Three Different Types of Strategic Alliances

Alliances are business relationships. They're about who you know in business, and like a personal network, they supplement your capabilities and weaknesses with strengths. Each alliance is a joint venture where two or more entities work together to achieve a shared goal while remaining separate and independent.

A strategic alliance goes a step further.

Strategic Alliance Definition:

It's a joint venture that bolsters a core business strategy, creates a competitive advantage, and abates competitors from moving in on a marketplace. It allows individual companies to achieve more together than they would have on their own.

Strategic alliances can take many different forms, but they often fall into three categories:

Joint Venture:

A joint venture is a child company of two parent companies. It's maintained by sharing resources and equity with a binding agreement. Whether it's formed for a specific purpose or an ongoing strategy, a joint venture has a clear objective, and profits are split between the two companies.

In 2016, Google's parent company Alphabet announced a joint venture with GlaxoSmithKline to research treating diseases with electrical signals. The joint venture, Galvani Bioelectronics, has continued to grow, bringing on more partners to build devices and further research in the emerging field of bioelectronics.

Equity Strategic Alliance:

An equity strategic alliance occurs when one company purchases equity in another business (partial acquisition), or each business purchases equity in each other (cross-equity transactions).

An example of an equity strategic alliance is Tesla's relationship with Panasonic. Their relationship began with a $30 million investment from Panasonic to accelerate battery technology for electric vehicles and grew to include building a lithium-ion battery plant in Nevada.

Non – Equity Strategic Alliance:

In a non-equity strategic alliance, organizations create an agreement to share resources without creating a separate entity or sharing equity. Non-equity alliances are often more loose and informal than a partnership involving equity. These make up the vast majority of business alliances.

Taking equity-sharing out of the equation can be a strategic advantage in research and development, production, and sales and marketing. In the previously mentioned example of Galvani Bioelectronics, there are many non-equity strategic alliances that have grown out of the original joint venture through Project Baseline. According to the Ivey Business Journal, a strategic business alliance needs five key components to be successful.

A successful Strategic Alliance:

1. It is critical to the success of a core business goal or objective.
2. It is critical to the development or maintenance of a core competency or other source of competitive advantage.
3. Blocks a competitive threat.
4. Creates or maintains strategic choices for the firm.
5. It mitigates a significant risk to the business.

If these things exist in the partnership, both organizations benefit from a symbiotic relationship that drives the business forward, staves off competition and threats, and establishes leadership in the marketplace.

As more and more businesses build their partner ecosystems, companies that do not actively build and maintain these relationships will flounder on their own, without the tools to be competitive in a global market.

Value Creation in Strategic Alliances
Strategic Alliances Create Value by:

1. Improving current operations
2. Changing the competitive environment
3. Ease of entry and exit

Current Operations are Improved Due to:

- Economies of scale from successful strategic alliances
- The ability to learn from the other partner(s)
- Risk and cost being shared between partner(s)

Changing the Competitive Environment through:

- Creating technology standards (for example, Sony and Panasonic announce to work together to produce a new-generation TV). This would help set a new standard in a competitive environment.

Easing entry and exit of companies through:

- A low-cost entry into new industries (a company can form a strategic partnership to easily enter into a new industry).
- A low-cost exit from industries (A new entrant can form a strategic alliance with a company already in the industry and slowly take over that company, allowing the company that is already in the industry to exit).

Challenges

Although strategic alliances create value, there are many challenges to consider:

- Partners may misrepresent what they bring to the table (lie about competencies that they do not have).
- Partners may fail to commit resources and capabilities to the other partners.
- One partner may commit heavily to the alliance while the other partner does not.
- Partners may fail to use their complementary resources effectively.

Advantages and Disadvantages of Strategic Alliances

Advantages of Strategic Alliances

Sharing Resources and Expertise: A strategic alliance should combine the best both companies have to offer. This can be a deeper understanding of the product, sales, or marketing knowledge, or even just more hands on deck to increase speed to market.

New-Market Penetration: In some cases, a strategic alliance gives access to new markets with a solution that wouldn't have been possible for either company on their own. For instance, companies going global often work with a trusted local partner to get an advantage in an emerging market.

Expanded Production: When it comes to manufacturing and distributing products, strategic alliances allow partners to increase their capabilities and scale quickly to meet demand.

Drive Innovation: With the right alliance, partners can outpace the competition with new solutions that are a complete package for their customers. These alliances are creative and revolutionary and change the market landscape in a dramatic way.

Strategic alliances allow partners to scale quickly, build innovative solutions for their customers, enter new markets, and pool valuable expertise and resources. And, in a business environment that values speed and innovation, this is a game-changer.

Disadvantages of strategic alliances

Loss of Control: In an alliance, both organizations must cede some control over how their business is run and perceived. A strategic alliance requires honesty and transparency, but that trust isn't built overnight. Without significant buy-in from both parties, an alliance may suffer.

Increased Liability: In a joint venture or equity strategic alliance, both companies are on the hook for the outcome. If something happens to stall production or create unhappy customers, both partners are at risk for the loss in reputation. For instance, in the case of Tesla and Panasonic, what was originally an advantageous relationship became fraught when batteries weren't produced and shipped quickly enough, causing delays in Tesla vehicle production and shipments. Reports now say that Tesla is putting its capital behind building its own battery technology to reduce dependence on Panasonic.

Strategic alliances can fail when partners misrepresent what they bring to the table, do not fully commit to the partnership, or fail to bring their resources together effectively.

MRS. POORNIMA G, ASSISTANT PROFESSOR IN COMMERCE, A J K
COLLEGE OF ARTS AND SCIENCE COIMBATORE

The "4C" Framework for Strategic Alliances:

Four elements are: Complementarities, Congruence of goals, Compatibility of organizations, and Change that will occur over the anticipated timeframe of the alliance. We now explore each of these elements in turn.

The management of strategic alliances has been more of an art than a science. They are often considered a less risky way to access new capabilities than M&A but alliances have their own pitfalls and firms that lack strong alliance capabilities are less likely to be able to create value with this mode. The management literature identifies indicators of such capabilities such as the presence of a dedicated alliance function (Prashant, Jeffrey, and Harbir, 2002).

Complementarities:

At the crux of any collaborative relationship is the notion that each party brings important resources and capabilities to the table. As such, the first step is to engage in a broad search for possible partners that have essential resources. A common mistake that firms make is to only look locally (e.g., within a given region) or through existing business relationships (Rosen Kopf and Almeida, 2003). In doing so, they may miss critical opportunities.

Congruent Goals:

Managers sometimes make the mistake of assuming that if a partner has strong complementary resources, they will have similar goals and benefit from an alliance. However, goal congruence is a very separate issue and this may be the most important area in which to dig deeper (Oxley and Sampson, 2004). For example, consider a small biotech firm that has developed a new compound and is considering licensing it to a larger Pharmaceutical firm that has capabilities to take the compound through trials and bring it to market.

Compatibility:

Once it is clear that a potential partner has complementary resources and goals are congruent, one might think that the deal is done. However, even two very willing partners might find it challenging to work together in the face of organizational or cultural incompatibilities.

Change:

This is often an overlooked factor. Alliances occur over a finite period and the conditions in each of the other 3C's (complementarities, congruent goals and compatibility) may shift over that timeframe.

For example, alliances have often been considered as learning races where each party seeks to learn important knowledge or capabilities from the other (Khanna, Gulati, and Nohria, 1998). Once the requisite learning has been achieved, the partner may withdraw from the alliance in spirit and perhaps even terminate the contract.

Learning shifts the complementarities so that the partners no longer need each other to the same extent. These changes in complementarities or other factors, such as new opportunities, may shift goal congruence as well.

Accordingly, it should be clear that an effective alliance capability would help a firm manage the 4Cs to identify the best alliance opportunities, form the best contracts to facilitate value creation and to manage the relationships over time and navigate any changes that do emerge (especially the end game).

3PL

Third-party logistics (abbreviated as 3PL, or TPL) in logistics and supply chain Management is an organization's use of third-party businesses to outsource elements of its distribution, warehousing, and fulfillment services.

A third party logistics company can store your inventory for you. It will pick, pack, and ship your products. 3PL is the vital link between your manufacturing operations and your customers. When your order fulfillment operations run smoothly, your customers are happy and your business grows. It's not an exaggeration to say that excellent fulfillment is the key to success for eCommerce companies.

Before you start working with a third-party logistics company, it's important to understand what 3PL is. This piece details how you can integrate third-party logistics into your operations, and how to find the best

What is Third-Party Logistics?

Third-party logistics, or 3PL, is used interchangeably with fulfillment warehouse or fulfillment center. Companies that provide 3PL services offer many of the same services as order fulfillment companies. These services include:

- Warehousing
- Inventory management
- Shipping and receiving
- FTL and LTL freight shipping
- Picking and packing
- Kitting and customization
- Reverse logistics (returns)

A third-party logistics company acts as an ecommerce fulfillment company. It provides all the services you need to outsource your logistics operations.

What is 3PL?

3PL stands for third-party logistics, described above. The term third-party logistics is often also used interchangeably with order fulfillment. A third-party warehouse provides a full range of ecommerce fulfillment services. This can include warehousing, order processing, and shipping and receiving. Many 3PL warehouses provide other services. These can include customer support, returns processing, and customization.

The 3PL business model is the most common type of outsourced logistics company. There are other types such as 4PL and 5PL, but by far most companies large and small are interested in 3PL.

Third Party Logistics (3PL) Basics:

Third-party logistics providers manage inbound and outbound transportation for their clients, as well as warehousing. Most 3PL companies own or lease warehouse space, which they provide to their clients. They generally don't own their own fleet of trucks but contract with other carriers for freight and shipping.

Third-Party Logistics Process

When you outsource your fulfillment, your products ship directly from the factory to the 3rd-party logistics warehouse. Once your inventory arrives, the third-party logistics company can provide a range of services. Here are just a few of the elements of the 3PL process.

Ecommerce Platform Integration

Most ecommerce businesses depend on multichannel selling to survive. To support this, your fulfillment warehouse needs strong IT. The best fulfillment companies integrate seamlessly with multiple sales platforms. Your provider should support all your sales channels or be able to create a custom API. In addition, you should be able to view and track the progress of your orders in real time online, via a dashboard.

FTL and LTL Freight Shipping And Receiving:

Full truckload (FTL) and less than truckload (LTL) freight can be essential tools to save you money on freight. This is particularly true if you often ship large orders to commercial customers or wholesale orders to retailers. You can also use freight services to ship your products between warehouses or to a distribution point closer to your customers. Your outsourced logistics company can guide you through this process. It can arrange for FTL or LTL loads and process incoming truckload freight. Your 3PL can also help you find the best deals and the right service level for your freight shipping.

Inventory Management:

When you work with a third-party logistics company, you no longer have to go it alone. Your 3rd-party logistics partner has valuable experience with inventory management. Your account rep can apply lessons learned from working with many e-commerce companies to help you manage your stock. Reach out for advice on restocking levels, supply chain management, and ideal seasonal inventory levels.

Picking, Packing, and Shipping:

Pick, pack, and ship services are the core of order fulfillment. When your customer places an order through one of your sales channels, it goes directly to your fulfillment warehouse. There, a picker finds the items for the order on the shelves. Then a packer selects the perfect box – not too big, not too little – and packages the order. The packer also applies the shipping label. Finally, the shipper makes sure the order gets picked up by the right carrier as soon as it's ready to go.

Same-Day Shipping:

Your third-party logistics provider may offer same-day shipping. This service means that your customer orders are picked, packed, and shipped on the same day they are received. There is usually a time cutoff for same-day shipping. For example, Red Stag Fulfillment offers two levels of same-day shipping service. One has a 3 PM cutoff; the other will ship orders that arrive as late as 5 PM on the same day. Same-day shipping gets your orders to your customers faster. And faster delivery leads to more satisfied customers.

Reverse Logistics:

Reverse logistics is a fancy term for returns. Returns are simply a fact of life in eCommerce. Your return rate will depend on a number of factors, including the type of merchandise you sell. Products that are sized, such as clothing and shoes, have much higher return rates than the industry average. Your eCommerce fulfillment company can accept and process returned items for you. The reverse logistics process includes examining returned items to assess whether they are damaged or can be returned to the shelf. Reverse logistics can also decrease the time it takes to make undamaged products available for purchase again.

Introduction to Advantages and Disadvantages of 3PL in Ecommerce Shipping

Anyone familiar with the world of ecommerce shipping knows how important third party logistics or 3PL is to the success of an online business. The advantages of 3PL are very commonly listed everywhere. From picking, packaging and delivery, third party logistics providers take care of the entire order fulfillment process for ecommerce businesses.

However, there are a few disadvantages of third-party logistics that online stores should also keep in mind when looking to hire a 3PL to manage shipping operations. The massive growth of ecommerce in India and worldwide has led to the mushrooming of numerous 3PLs. Which third-party logistics provider or 3PL is best for your e-commerce business will only come after a thorough understanding of how 3PL works in ecommerce shipping and logistics.

What is Third Party Logistics or 3PL

In ecommerce logistics, 3PL or third party logistics is the service provided by third party couriers and logistics software companies to ecommerce stores to help with their shipping and order delivery. Third-party logistics takes care of order procurement, storage, warehousing, stock management, labeling, picking, packing and finally delivering the order to the end customer. By choosing to work with a 3PL, online companies relegate the responsibility of shipping and order fulfillment on 3PL providers. Research shows, working alongside 3PLs helps ecommerce businesses to scale up much faster.

Most ecommerce companies start outsourcing shipping and logistics to third party logistics services because of the advantages they provide. As an online store grows and starts receiving a larger number of orders every month, it looks for a suitable 3PL to provide a smooth and streamlined shipping and delivery experience to its customers.

A third-party logistics provider can store items in its warehouses, manage stocks and replenish them when necessary and finally deliver the item when a customer places an order. Apart from these shipping services, a 3PL also provides customized packaging, picking, kitting, bundling, customs clearance, etc., for e-commerce retailers.

Advantages of 3PL or Third Party Logistics

The advantages of 3PL are immense. This is the reason why so many ecommerce companies all over the world choose to work with a third-party logistics provider. Some ecommerce companies while starting out decide to manage shipping in-house.

This is a viable option for a retailer when order volumes are low and logistics manageable. But as orders multiply over time, choosing to work with a 3PL is a good idea. Let's find out all the advantages that working with a third party logistics partner can provide e-commerce businesses.

Lower Shipping Prices:
One of the biggest advantages of 3PL is the cost-effectiveness it provides. Third-party logistics providers work with many different companies and for that reason, they can offer individual e- commerce companies much cheaper and more attractive shipping prices. Managing logistics in-house is an extremely costly investment. 3PL (3rd Party Logistics) companies on the other hand can make use of their economy of scale to provide beneficial shipping services at much lower rates.

Speedy Delivery:

Since 3PLs specialize in shipping services, they operate a large number of delivery fleets that can carry orders from one place to the other in a time-sensitive manner. Another advantage of third-party logistics is that they have several warehouses scattered all over the country.

Therefore, they are much better equipped to deliver orders faster to customers. Since Amazon normalized one-day delivery to customers, e-commerce third-party logistics providers have started offering lightning-fast deliveries to customers even at the shortest notice.

Warehouse Management:

Warehousing solutions are another major advantage offered by third-party logistic providers. For warehouse management, 3PL companies procure the entire stock of e-commerce companies and store it in several of their warehouses.

As soon as a customer places an order, third-party logistic providers rush to fulfill the order from the nearest warehouse to the customer. In this way, 3PLs not only take on the load of managing inventory but also make faster deliveries to customers. Young e-commerce companies strapped for space should definitely consider using warehouse management services offered by 3PLs.

Inventory Management:

Another benefit provided by third-partyE-commerce logistics is inventory management. Ecommerce companies can rely on 3PLs to manage their inventory, keep stock of which items are available, replenish stock as and when required, and also update inventory in case of product returns or exchanges.

In inventory management, all inventories is categorized in SKUs and stored in racks and bins in a warehouse. Most 3PLs will use a WMS (Warehouse Management Software) or OMS (Order Management Software) to automatically update inventory and display fresh stock on the e-commerce company's website or virtual marketplaces.

Real-Time Order Tracking:

A good order tracking feature is essential to maintaining transparency and communication between ecommerce companies and their customers. Today's consumers expect to know where their order is at all times.

To make this possible, third party logistics companies provide a self-serve order tracking page that can be easily accessed by customers by entering their Order Id or Tracking Number. A lot of 3PLs can even send order update notifications to customers on their Email and phones. By updating your customers about their orders where about ecommerce companies gain trust and brand loyalty.

Numerous Payment Gateways:

Third-party logistics providers can be super advantageous for the number of payment gateways they offer to customers. Lack of payment options in the checkout page is a big contributor to cart abandonment.

3PLs are equipped to handle cash payments like Cash on Delivery (COD), bank transfers, UPI, Credit/Debit cards and even Pay on Delivery options. Providing so many payment options to customers means fewer chances of cart abandonment and greater customer satisfaction at the time of purchase.

More Delivery Options:

Amazon Prime's Same Day Delivery has made e-commerce third-party logistics companies take notice. Since customers want faster deliveries than ever before, 3PLs have started offering same day, Next Day, 2-Hour, and hyper local delivery services to them. By tying up with a 3PL, e- commerce companies can reap these benefits provided by third party logistics. The faster the delivery the happier the customer. And everybody knows, happy customers are an asset to any business.

Increased Customer Satisfaction:

Customers like a hassle-free delivery. Third party logistics can provide that with their superior delivery fleets customized packaging, timely order status updates, and a safe transit of orders without damage or breakage. As e-commerce companies begin to grow out of their initial stages and scale up, they will want to enhance their customer satisfaction rate.

A higher customer retention rate means more and more customers return to your store, you receive fewer product returns and exchange requests and build a community of your people. The advantage of 3PL is that they can help online stores reach that phase much faster without having to shell out extra money to hire workforce and rent bigger warehouses.

Customized Shipping Services:

Customization and personalization is the key to reaching your customers' hearts. Third party logistic company's advantage is that they can provide a lot of customized shipping services for B2B and B2C sectors.

3PLs can also print customized shipping labels and create personalized packaging for special orders. Customized shipping services naturally come with added costs. Therefore, be sure to speak to your 3PL provider about extra charges beforehand.

Insurance and Other Benefits:

If your e-commerce store deals in Jewellery, precious stones, designer watches or any other valuable goods, you must prepare an insurance plan for shipping. The biggest advantage of third party logistics is that they have insurance plans to cover for any losses you might suffer in the case of any shipping mishap.

Insurance plans act as fail safe in the case of any unforeseen event. Make sure the insurance plan you choose does not make you the sole bearer of the loss. It's important to select a plan that puts the onus on both the parties.

Disadvantages of 3PL (Third Party Logistics)

The list above shows the many ways in which 3PLs can become an indispensable part of an e-commerce shipping operation. The advantage provided by third party logistics is so much that e-commerce stores often forget to look at the disadvantages that come with using third party logistics.

Although we agree that the disadvantages of 3PL are nothing compared to their advantage, it's still worth something to look into. Directly contracting with carriers has a lot of fringe benefits that can help you push and shove your way to the front of the pack. However, juggling multiple courier partners comes with its own range of obstacles that have to be considered. Below, is the list of 3PL (Third Party Logistics) disadvantages that every Ecommerce company should look into before hiring one for their business.

Difficulty Tracking Multi-Carrier Orders:

This is one of the major difficulties that you'll encounter when you're directly tying up with multiple courier partners. Being able to track your orders is a supremely important part of the e-commerce process. Without being able to efficiently keep an eye on the movement and status of orders placed on a wide-scale level, things can get pretty chaotic! This can be a disadvantage of 3PL that many e-commerce companies face.

Separate Allocation of Orders:

Another disadvantage of 3PL is that once an order is placed, allocating and assigning a courier partner to fulfill that order doesn't seem like a big task. However, if you're tied up with 5 courier partners, each may be assigned anywhere between 20 to 50 orders per day, depending on their serviceability. You'll be entirely dependent on customers and the courier partners to inform you of any delivery exceptions.

Independent Communications:

Each carrier has to be reached out to separately in case of any issues with an order. While the speed of communication may now be unhindered by a middleman, it is an inconvenient and time-consuming process to reach out to each carrier independently to deal with individual order issues.

Without making use of API integrations to reach out to them in a more streamlined manner, miscommunications can also occur. This again is the disadvantage of using third party logistics for shipping operations.

Carrier Performances Monitored Separately:

There's a major consequence to orders being tracked and managed with each carrier independently. The performance of each courier partner also has to be analyzed separately based entirely on inputs provided by each carrier. And whatever metrics and analytics you have resources for.

Separate Carrier Platforms:

The biggest barrier to monitoring carrier performance is that each courier partner maintains separate websites or back ends for tracking the status of orders. This means that the data required to monitor each carrier's performance has to be individually pulled by you from each carrier's respective website. This can be another disadvantage of using third party logistics companies.

Different SLA Terms:

Given the wide range of pin codes that you need to service and the variety of specialized services you'll make use of, each carrier demands a separate focus from you. This goes doubly when it comes to creating SLA terms. Absolute clarity of your operations and necessities is required at this point. Having different SLA terms can be a disadvantage of working with third- party logistics partners.

While some terms may be standard, the advantages of working with different carriers can only be enjoyed when you negotiate the best terms. This means knowing what you want from each of them, be it access to remote areas, better product safety in transit, or discounted rates. A lack of preparation can result in more hidden costs and less utilization of necessary services.

Different Terminology Used by Carriers:

When it comes to relationships, be them with your customers, your courier partners or your significant other, communication is key. All it takes is one misspoken word to completely ruin your dinner plans. Similarly, the entire delivery process for each order can be shaken with just a few misprints or alternate phrasing.

No Standardized Shipping Labels or Packaging:

Customized shipping labels and packaging are a great way to raise brand loyalty and keep customers thinking about you. There's a reason why McDonald's puts its iconic giant yellow M everywhere it gets the opportunity, on every to-go bag and every burger wrapper.

A uniform process and template for shipping labels also reduce the likelihood of any possible confusion during transit. However, most of the top courier companies maintain their own shipping labels so each customer receives a shipment with a different label, making them less likely to identify with your brand.

No Standardized Customer Communications:

There's nothing more exciting for an online shopper than receiving a message that says their order is on the way. However, these messages are usually drafted by carriers who tend to use their own phrasing and language. The same customer may end up placing an initial order that's delivered by Carrier A and then a second-order delivered by Carrier B.

This may be because he/she/they requested express delivery or some service which is only offered by Carrier B to that location. Carrier A may say an order is first "dispatched", then "in- transit", then finally "on the way" to the customer. Carrier B, however, first says when the order has been "picked up", after which it is "on the way", and then finally "out for delivery". The result is a very confusing barrage of messages that leaves the customer wondering what each message means and where their order actually is.

Benefits of Third-Party Logistics

There are several benefits of this operational model.

- **Lower Cost of Goods Sold:** When you purchase products upfront, you will pay the wholesale price. The more you buy, the lower your costs and the higher your profit margins.

- **Greater Flexibility in Product Sourcing:** When you use an eCommerce fulfillment business model, you can more easily source products from more than one manufacturer. All your items will be stored in the same warehouse, so orders that include products from multiple suppliers can ship in the same box. This saves on shipping costs.
- **More Control Over your Logistics Operations:** You get to choose an order fulfillment partner that provides the services your customers expect.
- **Faster Order Fulfillment.** You can pick a third-party logistics service with warehouse locations that will get your orders delivered quickly.
- **Easier Returns Processing.** The 3rd-party logistics warehouse that shipped your products can provide customer service and seamlessly process any returns. This improves customer satisfaction and lets you put products back into inventory quickly.

Supplier Partnership

Partnering is a defined as a continuing relationship, between a buying firm and supplying firm, involving a commitment over an extended time period, an exchange of information, and acknowledgement of the risks and rewards of the relationship.

What are the Five Benefits of Good Supplier Relationships?

Here are just some of the benefits of having a solid relationship with your suppliers:

- Timely Delivery of Quality Materials. ...
- Smooth-sailing Production. ...
- Customer Satisfaction. ...
- More Business for You. ...
- Take Advantage of Great Deals. ...
- Excellent Support. ...
- Saves Your Company Money.

What are the Advantages of Supplier Partnerships?

That's where supplier relationship management has its advantages.

- Lower Costs. When it comes to seeking out and negotiating fresh deals with new suppliers, there are a number of initial costs involved. ...
- Improved Efficiency. ...
- Consolidated Supply Chain. ...
- Outsourcing Activities. ...
- Ongoing Improved Operations. ...
- Wrap Up.

Factors to Consider When Forming a Supplier Partnership

When it comes to achieving growth and success in the supply chain, one of the most important strategies is establishing and maintaining supplier partnerships that are built on trust and transparency. The pandemic has sparked a significant shift in how suppliers engage with one another. For some, relationships have flourished, as both parties have worked together to respond effectively to mitigate risk. For others, it has made them rethink who they work with. To make sure you get the most value from your supplier partnership in 2023 read these factors to consider.

Pricing vs Quality:

Suppliers must offer a fair price for the product, but it is good practice to always negotiate. It is worth considering that low price does not always mean low quality, just as a high price does not necessarily indicate a high level of quality. If the quality of your supplier's product or service is poor, you will inevitably incur extra costs for your time, returns and replacements. You will also risk losing business with any delays that result. If you decide to pass poor quality on to your customers, you risk damaging your business reputation for the long term. Find a balance between price & quality when forming a supplier partnership.

Use of Technology:

How suppliers utilize technology can provide good insight into their flexibility and ability to adapt to new opportunities. For example, <u>rebate management software</u> with built in collaboration can facilitate the information exchange between parties to allow more time to focus on future strategic opportunities and risks surrounding your deals.

Scalability:

Make sure that your supplier partnership has the capacity to scale and deliver in line with your projected future requirements. For example, determine how flexible the supplier is when it comes to providing small quantity and high-volume orders. If you grow to require extremely large shipments of the product over time, you could quickly outgrow your original supplier selection. Knowing what the growth pattern is for the product you are sourcing before selecting a supplier will allow you to form a supplier partnership that can scale to meet your changing requirements.

Trust & Stability:

Strategic sourcing and procurement recognize the importance of identifying and mitigating potential risks in a supplier partnership. Always make sure your supplier is trustworthy and look for experienced suppliers who have been in business a long time. It's in your best interest that your supplier stays in business to prevent disruptions to your operation. Do your homework and check each vendor's financial health and stability before doing business with them long-term. The reputation of its supplier can sometimes be decisive in the final customer's purchase decision.

Supplier Performance:

The last thing you want to do is to form a supplier partnership with someone who is unreliable. Make sure you pay attention to their performance. You need to know that the supplier you're working with will be able to provide the level of service your company needs. If the supplier keeps delivering orders late or low-quality, these are red flags.

Communication and Accessibility:

Almost two-thirds (64%) of enterprises don't have strong communication channels in place with suppliers, according to a __survey by HICX__. This reiterates the importance of clear communication channels when proactively seeking a supplier partnership. The best suppliers take the initiative to talk to you regularly in order to determine ways to serve you better and support your long-term goals. You need to be certain that when you call, you'll get an answer within a reasonable amount of time. The last thing you want is to have any disruptions because of a lack of communication.

Location:

The location of the supplier can have a significant impact on how you work with them. If your supplier is in a different country than you, this can offer potential cost savings, however they are not the right choice if you require small quantities, short lead times or flexibility. With the ongoing disruptions to the supply chain and material shortages it may be worth looking locally for a supplier partnership. For example, according to **Thomas net**, 83% of manufacturers said they intend to find North American suppliers in 2021 — up from 54% before the pandemic lockdowns of 2020.

DISTRIBUTOR INTEGRATION

An integrated business model is when the vendor provides transportation and distribution; warehousing and value-added services all bundled into a single contract. Integrated supply chain management refers to an enterprise resource planning approach to supply chain management. A business facilitates relationships with all of its suppliers and manages all distribution and logistics activities through a centralized system rather than having multiple systems within the organization.

Step 1 – Cleaning Up of the Master Data:

Before the process of DMS implementation starts, an organization needs to check its master data for any redundant data, which can often be found in the form of inactive SKUs and parties that the organization is no longer in business with! Only when there is no such futile information in the systems can the new Distributor Management System properly takes effect!

Step 2 – ERP Integration:

This can be easily termed as one of the most crucial stages of DMS implementation. While ERP integration with the DMS process might seem cumbersome to begin with, it is quintessential to the compliance of Distributor Management System, as it allows the much-needed access to critical data including but not limited to – primary sales, primary orders, new vendor creation, and new client creation.

Step 3 – Create your Invoice Template:

Standardizing your invoice template will enable you to save precious time by sending out system-generated invoices, while also eliminating any room for error. Moreover, it will also help you keep a track of the invoicing systems that your distributors are following.

Step 4 – Incentivize Distributors:

It is now time for you to offer incentives to distributors, as a way to encourage them to use the DMS platform. Right from encouraging new digital behaviors to promptly setting distributor claims, and even adopting future technologies, this stage will make it all easy and approachable for you.

Step 5 – Reward Compliance:

Driving change amongst distributors is no easy task and requires a strategic approach. While there will be a few distributors who will happily dial the boat with you, most will resist. An easy way to get them on board is by creating a plan to rewards distributors who choose DMS compliance.

Step 6 – Ensure Post-Implementation Upkeep:

While the process of installation of DMS in itself sits well with companies, it is the post-installation upkeep that many organizations struggle with. That said, with the help of a reliable customer support team from the Distributor Management System provider's step, it can become rather convenient to follow the below-mentioned tips.

Data Entry of Products and Related Aspects

As important as it is to clear any old and redundant data, it is equally important to update the software with the complete data pertaining to every product, distributor, warehouse and so on. This ensures quick and easy access to these crucial details, while also enabling automated order processing. Moreover, it brings the entire process to an optimal speed, which may not be possible if the requisite data is absent from the system.

Automation of Order Processing:

While it may seem time-consuming at the very start, but once all the requisite details have been entered into the system it becomes extensively convenient to automate the entire process right from getting orders to confirming them, from creating delivery Challan to applying for promotions and generating invoices. Needless to say, this helps save a significant amount of time and resources, which could be rather invested in adding value to the customers' bottom line.

Integration of Accounting Systems with the Distributor Management System:

Keeping a track of the payment to be received from retailers, credit limit, credit history, and other minute details can become as easy as ABC, simply by integrating the existing accounting system with the DMS. This will not only help ensure that all payments are received in full by a stipulated date, but also encourage retailers to make timely payments.

CHAPTER IV

PROCUREMENT AND OUTSOURCING

Procurement and Outsourcing: Outsourcing – Benefits and Risks – Framework for Make/Buy Decision – e-Procurement – Frame Work of e-Procurement.

Procurement outsourcing is the transfer of specified key procurement activities relating to sourcing and supplier management to a third party. Typically, the most common outsourced activities are indirect materials and services that are commonly referred to as indirect procurement. The most challenging task for a Procurement professional is getting his procurement terminology right in order to define his scope of work. The pain area is, these terms are often used interchangeably. Though it's a fact that these terms mean the same, but they can't be used interchangeably.

One of the very good examples of this is "Purchasing", the term Purchasing is used as a synonym to procurement but, holds a different meaning altogether under procurement industry. As a result, such variations can hinder the effective communications among the businesses. The concern at the top level is unless we understand the basics of procurement; we wouldn't be able to effectively communicate our scope of work. So, here in this article, we pen down some key terms or Procurement concepts that would help you get your procurement terminology right.

What is Procurement?

Procurement is a business management function. Procurement is essentially an acquisition of products and services, especially for the business purpose. It covers a complete range of activities from identifying the need of goods and services to its allotment. In a broader sense if we talk, Procurement involves activities like;

1)Selecting vendors

2)Establishing payment terms

3)Negotiating Contracts

4)Regulatory compliance

5)Analysis and sourcing

Thus, procurement is an umbrella term under which Purchasing is just a component. Since procurement is an umbrella term and includes all the core business activities, it should be considered an important corporate activity. Coming to Purchasing, **Purchasing** is a subset of Procurement. Though these terms are being used interchangeably they mean different. Purchasing simply involves buying and selling of the goods and services. Purchasing is only restricted to receiving and making payments. Purchasing can be best known as the transaction-oriented function of Procurement.

Sourcing, as the name implies, is a finding a source from where the goods and services can be procured. It is a subsection of the procurement, where, procurement is concerned with acquiring of goods and services, sourcing are finding a least expensive supplier for those goods. Since the business profits heavily rely on finding the best source of suppliers it is considered to be the first step taken by the business before its first sale. These are the some of the basic concepts of the procurement used in the business world and by getting a fair idea of the differences in the procurement terminology, will help us enhance the understand ability of the procurement industry and stop letting us from using these terms interchangeably to avoid any miscommunication.

OUTSOURCING

Outsourcing is the business practice of hiring a party outside a company to perform services or create goods that were traditionally performed in-house by the company's own employees and staff. Outsourcing is a practice usually undertaken by companies as a cost-cutting measure. As such, it can affect a wide range of jobs, ranging from customer support to manufacturing to the back office. Outsourcing was first recognized as a business strategy in 1989 and became an integral part of business economics throughout the 1990s. The practice of outsourcing is subject to considerable controversy in many countries. Those opposed argue that it has caused the loss of domestic jobs, particularly in the manufacturing sector. Supporters say it creates an incentive for businesses and companies to allocate resources where they are most effective, and that outsourcing helps maintain the nature of free-market economies on a global scale.

- Companies use outsourcing to cut labour costs, including salaries for their personnel, overhead, equipment, and technology.
- Outsourcing is also used by companies to dial down and focus on the core aspects of the business, spinning off the less critical operations to outside organizations.
- On the downside, communication between the company and outside providers can be hard, and security threats can amp up when multiple parties can

access sensitive data.

The Benefits of outsourcing often include one or more of the following:

- Lower costs (due to economies of scale or lower labour rates)
- Increased efficiency
- Variable capacity
- Increased focus on strategy/core competencies
- Access to skills or resources
- Increased flexibility to meet changing business and commercial conditions
- Accelerated time to market
- Lower ongoing investment in internal infrastructure
- Access to innovation, intellectual property, and thought leadership
- Possible cash influx resulting from transfer of assets to the new provider

Benefits of Outsourcing Supply Chain Management

Supply chain processes that can be outsourced to a qualified 3PL:

- Order fulfillment
- Warehouse receiving
- Product storage and shipping
- Order management
- Inventory management
- Automated shipping

- Returns management

Now that we have a better understanding of why outsourcing fulfillment can help a business and which processes you can outsource, let's look at seven of the top reasons for outsourcing your supply chain management.

Strategic Positioning:

A major reason many companies outsource their supply chain management is to position the company more strategically. Outsourcing supply chain services allows you to focus on activities that are core to your business. When you stop worrying about storeroom operations or order management, you can focus on sales and marketing, product development, and other areas that improve your competitive advantage.

The aim of any business is to find a market position that is both profitable and defendable in its markets of choice, and such a position can only be achieved through differentiated products or lower relative costs, that is, by either serving different needs from competitors, or serving the same needs in different ways.A market position that is both profitable and defendable can only be achieved through differentiated value and a distinctive value chain.

Increased Value:

Outsourcing supply chain functions increases value to your customers by allowing your company to become more efficient and nimble in areas like order picking and packing. This allows you to deliver products and services faster and with more accuracy, which cuts down on returns and lost sales from frustrated customers. Streamlined operations allow a business to better meet customer demand, and happy customers are loyal customers.

Reduced Operational Cost:

Outsourcing supply chain management provides you with greater flexibility in controlling your costs. You can choose a contract that matches the current level of services required by your business. As your business scales up or down, you can adjust the scope of work covered by the contract so you pay only for what you need.

Improved Ability to Meet Customer Demand:

A 3PL with the right systems in place can better help you manage inventory levels, predict demand through sales trends, and respond quickly to customer needs. Having such functions outsourced to a logistics company reduces the chances of an inefficient supply chain, which can seriously damage customer relations and profitability. The human resources, technology, and effective processes that 3PL suppliers can offer better ensure all supply chain processes go smoothly and efficiently.

Flexibility:

A 3PL offers a high degree of flexibility, as they aren't limited by fixed assets like warehouses or transportation equipment. Normally, this would require a large capital investment for a business to purchase or lease them and would come with a fixed cost regardless of utilization level or fluctuating inventory levels.

Increased Working Resources:

A 3PL logistics provider allows a company to increase its resources without having to hire additional staff or purchase more equipment at high costs. In fact, some may even specialize in areas where your business lacks expertise, such as warehousing software systems or IT infrastructure management systems.

Peace of Mind:

Peace of mind is one of the top reasons for outsourcing supply chain management. Knowing you're partnering with a fulfillment company that's an expert in supply chain management can help you worry about one less thing.

RISKS of outsourcing include:

- Slower turnaround time
- Lack of business or domain knowledge
- Language and cultural barrier
- Time zone differences lack of control

Risks of Outsourcing Supply Chain Management

Although outsourcing SCM has a considerable number of benefits, there are just as many Risks.

Quality may Suffer:

Your SCM partner should have extensive knowledge of your products or services. Otherwise, the quality of your offerings may diminish. This risk is increased when the third-party company tries to cut corners or use cheaper materials. Such practices can be detrimental to your company and may significantly reduce sales, alongside your brand equity, so avoid using SCM partners who don't prioritize quality.

You could Face Setbacks:

Outsourcing SCM can become a complicated process that opens up more chances for setbacks. Watch out for unrealistic timelines that could cause revenue loss and more issues down the supply chain.

There may be Integration Challenges:

Watch out for solutions that have a long on boarding process. The business operations become smooth once a business is integrated with the SCM partner, but the transition process can be a nightmare. It requires both parties to invest a considerable amount of time, and it also requires a good financial backing. If either party slacks, then it can cause delays and several mishaps. Several problems are likely to arise during the transition phase because this stage requires better communication besides time and money.

There could be Unexpected Costs:

Occasionally, taxes, shipping costs, and other hidden fees may get out of control. Some 3PLs have multiple hidden costs, such as labeling, pick and pack, boxing, and more. To avoid this, work with providers that are transparent with their costs so you can protect your profit margins.

Framework for Make-Or-Buy Decision

A make-or-buy decision refers to an act of using cost-benefit to make a strategic choice between manufacturing a product in-house or purchasing from an external supplier. It arises when a producing company faces a diminishing capacity, experiences problems with the current suppliers, or sees changing demand. Also referred to as an outsourcing decision, a make-or-buy decision compares the costs and benefits associated with producing a necessary good or service internally to the costs and benefits involved in hiring an outside supplier for the resources in question. To compare costs accurately, a company must consider all aspects regarding the acquisition and storage of the items versus creating the items in-house, which may require the purchase of new equipment, as well as storage costs.

Benefits of a Make-or-Buy Decision

A make-or-buy decision framework relates to autonomy, and a company selects from the many advanced options to account for various factors associated with outsourcing.

Lower Costs and Higher Capital Investments:
One of the most notable advantages that a company enjoys when embracing a make-or-buy decision approach is that it can lower costs and increase capital investments, regardless of whether it decides to make materials in-house or subcontract from an external vendor.

Source of Competitive Advantage:
A rigorous make-or-buy analysis can also act as a source of competitive advantage. For example, a company can increase the value it delivers to customers and shareholders from its core service and skills. It can also stay flexible by adopting a make-or-buy decision approach.

Such a company is better placed to weather the storm of a market downturn. To realize the benefits, companies must consider the internal and external environment in which they operate. In particular, the culture in which such decisions are reached, and the agenda of the parties involved can influence the decisions and their implementation, as well as the sustainability of the policy.

Process of Make or Buy Decision:
A make-or-buy decision refers to an act of using cost-benefit to make a strategic choice between manufacturing a product in-house or purchasing from an external supplier. It arises when a producing company faces a diminishing capacity, experiences problems with the current suppliers, or sees changing demand.

E-PROCUREMENT

Electronic procurement, also known as e-procurement or supplier exchange, is the process of requisitioning, ordering and purchasing goods and services online. It is a business-to-business process. Unlike e-commerce, e-procurement utilizes a supplier's closed system and is only available to registered users.

E-Procurement, also known as electronic procurement or supplier exchange, is the purchase and sale of supplies, equipment, works, and services through a web interface or other networked system.

The technology is designed to centralize and automate interactions between an organization, customers, and other value chain partners to improve the speed and efficiency of procurement practices.

We distinguish between the following forms

- e-ordering;
- web-based ERP;
- e-sourcing;
- e-tendering;
- e-reverse auctioning;
- E-informing.

What is e-procurement?

Electronic procurement, also known as e-procurement or supplier exchange, is the process of requisitioning, ordering, and purchasing goods and services online. It is a business-to-business business process.

Unlike e-commerce, e-procurement utilizes a supplier's closed system and is only available to registered users. E-procurement facilitates interactions between preferred suppliers and customers through bids, purchase orders, and invoices.

E-procurement started in the 1980s, following the development of Electronic Data Interchange (EDI). A decade later, improvements in EDI allowed organizations to develop online catalogs for vendors. Today, e-procurement involves everything from supplier evaluation and selection to contract management, electronic orders, and payments.

E-procurement uses a web interface or some other kind of networked system that connects suppliers and customers. In the enterprise, a chief procurement officer or procurement department usually sets the policies governing the e-procurement of materials for the organization.

The goal of using an e-procurement system is to acquire products or services at the best possible price and at the best possible time. To meet this objective, it's important for businesses to establish relationships with suppliers. This enables procurement personnel to negotiate contracts with suppliers. They can also set guidelines or limits around budgets and spending within the e-procurement platform.

How does e-procurement work?

E-procurement eliminates the need to manually carry out laborious, procurement-related tasks such as auctions and eTenders, exchanging supplier contracts, and filling out supplier onboarding questionnaires. The process works by connecting various entities and processes through a centralized platform. Vendor management/supplier management is one of the most important aspects of e-procurement. It involves both supplier relationship management and supplier information management.

Other key components in e-procurement include the following:

- **e-sourcing:** requirements definition and pre-qualifying potential suppliers;
- **e-tendering:** request for information, proposals, and quotations;
- **e-auctioning:** evaluating suppliers, negotiation, and contract management;
- **e-ordering and payment:** creating requisitions and purchase orders, and receiving ordered items; and
- Analytics: view spending and takes corrective measures as required.

Finally, e-informing is vital in the e-procurement process. It involves a two-way exchange of information between all parties involved in the process to generate mutually beneficial outcomes.

The E-Procurement Process

The e-procurement process corresponds with the traditional procurement cycle. There are five main digital processes involved in e-procurement. These processes coincide with traditional procurement cycle stages: requirement definition, sourcing, solicitation, evaluation, contracting, and contract management.

E-Informing:
E-informing coincides with all stages of the traditional procurement cycle. It also overlaps with all digital

processes of e-procurement. E-informing involves a two-way exchange of proprietary information. The exchange occurs between internal parties within the organization and with external parties, allowing the organization to optimize its e-procurement processes.

E-Sourcing:

E-sourcing is the initial phase of e-procurement, coinciding with requirement definition and sourcing. It involves pre-qualifying potential suppliers based on the procuring company's requirements to shortlist vendors for the evaluation stage.

E-Tendering:

E-tendering coincides with solicitation and evaluation. It involves requesting information, proposals, and quotations from the shortlisted vendors. This helps the procuring organization with analyzing and assessing the suppliers. In this stage, the procuring organization uses tools to ensure transparency during selection.

E-Auctioning or E-Reverse Auctioning:

E-auctioning or e-reverse auctioning is associated with evaluation and contracting. In this stage, the parties involved negotiate pricing and contract terms. After reaching an agreement, the procuring organization buys the goods or services from the vendor.

In e-auctioning, many buyers compete to contract with one supplier by offering higher prices. However, in e-reverse auctioning, many suppliers compete to contract with one buyer by underbidding.

E-Ordering:

E-ordering coincides with the contracting and contract management stages. It involves creating and approving requisitions, placing orders, and receiving the ordered items. In this stage, completed on-call contracts are indexed in a digital catalog. Employees can access this catalog and place an order at any time.

7-Step Procurement Process

- Assess your company's outsourcing needs.
- Compare outsourced market options.
- Use strategic sourcing to choose your suppliers.
- Choose supplier and negotiate contract terms.
- Implementation and integration of vendor collaboration.
- Review vendor performance.
- Keep accurate records of vendor invoices.

Benefits of E-Procurement Reduced costs

Digital procurement processes eliminate errors associated with handling paperwork and manual orders. The procurement department can focus more on strategic sourcing and less on redundant tasks like processing purchase orders and invoices. E-procurement results in lower administrative costs and overhead for the procuring organization. It also enables competitive sourcing and increases cost savings.

E-procurement lets businesses match online invoices with purchase orders (2-way matching), and also receive reports (3-way matching), if applicable to the purchase transaction. This saves significant payables time and reduces costs.

Enhanced Spending Control:

E-procurement lets businesses more effectively track spending, purchasing budgets, and incoming deliveries. E-procurement solutions usually provide dashboards that track these metrics in real time. Companies reduce maverick spending (tail spending) and improve spend management. These systems also generate purchase reports that help businesses lower supplier fraud.

Improved Transparency and Visibility:

E-procurement improves transparency and visibility across all procurement processes by enhancing information sharing. Companies can decentralize procurement processes (sourcing and approval, purchase requisition and order, delivery and receipt, and invoice verification and payment) and centralize their strategic procurement processes (product specification, procurement planning, supplier selection, request for quotation, assessment of quotes, and negotiation) to significantly improve supply chain efficiency.

Saved Time:

E-procurement platforms automate redundant activities such as purchase order tracking, supplier evaluation, invoice processing and matching, and requests for documents such as proposals and quotations. Employees can access and browse online catalogs of the company's approved preferred suppliers from anywhere. As a result, approvers can authorize purchase orders at any moment, reducing turnaround time.

Improved Internal and External Relations:

E-procurement software improves information sharing across internal departments and with external stakeholders. It provides an information repository to store vendor details, purchase reports, transaction history, supplier contracts, etc. End users can more easily identify and prioritize products based on their requirements and compare items from several suppliers simultaneously with e-purchasing.

Framework of E-Procurement:

The e-procurement value chain consists of indent management, e-Informing, e-Tendering, e-Auctioning, vendor management, catalogue management, purchase order integration, Order Status, Ship Notice, e-invoicing, e-payment, and contract management. Indent management is the workflow involved in the preparation of tenders.

Types of e-procurement Models

E-commerce trading between organizations usually occurs as part of the procurement process, which is part of the broader business activities of supply chain management. 'Procurement' refers to all activities involved with obtaining items from a supplier, this includes purchasing, but also inbound logistics such as transportation, goods-in and warehousing before the item is used. Online this process is known as e-procurement.

Knudsen (2003) and Smart (2010) have reviewed simple classification of different types or applications of e-procurement. These are the main types:

E-Sourcing: Finding potential new suppliers using the internet during the information gathering step of the procurement process.

E-Tendering: The process of screening suppliers and sending suppliers requests for information (RFI) and requests for price (RFP)

E-Informing: Qualification of suppliers for suitability. It doesn't involve transaction but instead handles information about the supplier's quality financial status or delivery capabilities.

E-reverse Auctions: Enable the purchasing company to buy goods and services that have the lowest price or combination of lowest price and other conditions via internet technology.

E-MRO and web-based ERP

These involve the purchase and supply of products which are the core of the most e-Procurement applications. The software used manages the process of creating and approving purchasing requisitions, placing orders and receiving goods or service ordered.

Smart (2010) also reviewed the business benefits of e-procurement through case studies of three companies. He identified five key drivers or supplier selection criteria for e-procurement adoption related to improving:

Control – Improving compliance, achieving centralization, raising standards, optimizing sourcing strategy and improved auditing data. Enhanced budgetary control is achieved through rules to limit spending and improved reporting facilities.

Cost – Improved buying leverage through increased supplier competition, monitoring savings targets and transactional cost reduction.

Process – Rationalizing and standardization of e-procurement process giving reduced cycle time, improved visibility of processes for management and efficient invoice settlement.

Individual Performance – Knowledge sharing, value-added productivity and productivity improvements.

Supplier management – Reduced supplier numbers, supplier management and selection and integration.

MRS. POORNIMA G, ASSISTANT PROFESSOR IN COMMERCE, A J K
COLLEGE OF ARTS AND SCIENCE COIMBATORE

Process efficiencies result in less staff time spent in searching and ordering products and reconciling deliveries with invoices so potentially leading to reduced costs of employees can be reassigned. Savings also occur due to automated validation of pre-approved spending budgets for individuals and departments, leading to fewer people processing each order, and in less time. It is also possible to reduce the cost of physical materials such as specially printed order forms and invoices.

CHAPTER V

DIMENSION OF CUSTOMER VALUE

Dimension of Customer Value – Conformance of Requirement – Product Selection – Price and Brand – Value Added Services – Strategic Pricing – Smart Pricing – Customer Value Measures

Customer Value is created along three different dimensions: Functionality (the job that the solution does and how well it does it), Reliability (how consistent the solution is at doing the job well) and Convenience (how accessible the solution is to customers and how easy it is to use).

CONFORMANCE REQUIREMENTS

Conformance requirements are the expression, in the form of a statement, which conveys the criteria to be fulfilled [ISO Guide 2]. The conformance requirements are stated in a conformance clause or statements within the specification.

PRODUCT SELECTION

Product Selection and Development Process are very complex process, which begins with idea generation and continues till commercialization. The process requires coordination between various departments. The process can be broken up into the following stages:

Criteria for Product Selection

Selecting/choosing the appropriate product or service can be considered the important building block of every business venture.

As a matter of fact, products serve the business as the most important and visible first contacts with buyers i.e. end users. The physical nature of products to the consumers typifies the psychological symbols of personal attributes, goal and strategic pathways. In other words, consumers are most likely to form opinion and perspectives for the entrepreneur.

Factors Responsible for Selection of Product Supply- Demand Gap

The size and scope of the potential and unsatisfied market demand, which forms the bedrock of business opportunity, will dictate, to great proportions, the need to settle for a particular product. One rule of thumb in developing a product selection criteria template is that the product with the most frequency of need/demand possesses the greater chance of bestowing success on the business, and should be selected. In plain terms, there must be existing demand (a market) for the chosen product.

Financing:

The size of the funds that can be accessed is another important consideration in choosing a method of product selection permitted. Adequate funding is required to carry out pre-launch activities such as the development, production, promotion, marketing, and distribution amongst others, of the selected product.

Availability of and Access to Starter Materials:

Differences in products require different starter materials. Factors such as the source of the materials, the quality to be achieved as well as the quantity of the raw materials are key management decisions. Will the raw materials be available in sufficient quantities, on a continual basis? Where are the locations of raw materials needed? Are they accessible? Will it be important to situate the business close to these sources of raw materials? In the event of local sources being incapable of meeting demand, are there viable alternatives abroad? The entrepreneur must embark on a thorough analysis of these limiting factors before settling for a particular product for a market.

Technical Considerations:

The production route for the product bears a lot of weight when it comes to product selection process in entrepreneurship. The technical dynamics of the chosen product on the existing production line will be x-rayed against factors such as available technology, power requirement and even the use of automated processes or human labor.

In addition, the choice of a particular product may warrant either the acquisition of new equipment or refurbishing of used machinery. The product must also be deemed technically satisfactory to the user.

Profit Viability/Marketability:

As is often the case, the product that meets the criterion of giving the optimum return on investment, will be selected. However, a product may be chosen on the ground that it utilizes dormant capacity or helps with the sales of existing products. The product must also bear the important characteristic of being marketable.

Qualified and Skilled Personnel:

Qualified personnel will be required to handle the production and marketing, on an ongoing basis. The cost associated with manufacturing the product must be kept to the barest minimum by reducing wastage. This is achievable through the engagement of competent and skilled hands.

Government Policies and Objectives:

These product selection factors are often beyond the control of the entrepreneur. The thrust of government policies on economics and commerce, over time, is usually in the national interest, which may or may not be at odds with the objectives of the business. For instance, the insistence of government on the use of 100% locally sourced starter materials will greatly influence the decisions of a business with regard to what business product to introduce to the market.

Standard global practices advocate identifying a number of criteria upon which product selection can be carried out. Scores can be allocated to each criterion to come up with an objective evaluation.

What are the Phases Involved in New Product Selection Exercise

After knowing the criteria to select a product in entrepreneurship, what are the stages involved? Three basic stages are involved in new product selection process. These sum up to idea generation and synthesis; evaluation and choice. These are the practical product selection steps and stages that you should know.

Idea Generation and Synthesis:

Medical product ideas and other investment opportunities originate from different sources such as financial newspapers and journals, research papers, consulting firms, chambers of commerce and industry, universities, competitors.

The origin for idea generation could be a simple analysis of the concept of S.W.O.T (Strengths, Weaknesses, Opportunities and Threats). Ideas could also be developed through brainstorming, research and business think tanks.

Evaluation:

Screening of the product ideas is the bedrock of evaluation. Considerations include the potential value of the product, cost of time and money, equipment required, suitability of potential product in the long term financial objectives of the business, presence of qualified personnel in the production and marketing processes, need thorough consideration.

A pre-feasibility study of the product market, technical and financial aspect should be embarked upon at the early stages, in order to come up with the consequent benefits and associated cost implications. A pre-feasibility serves as the fore-runner to a feasibility study, although it less detailed. A pre-feasibility study will analyse large and complex product start-ups before a proper feasibility study is made. This is vital to understanding product selection.

Choice:

A choice is reached for a product, which has scaled the hurdles and has been found to be commercially viable, technically feasible and economically desirable. At this stage in this **product selection guide**, resources and manpower can then be deployed to launch the product into the market.

PRICE AND BRAND

Product Pricing is a pricing strategy in which the by-products of a process are also sold separately at a specific price so as to earn additional revenue from the same infrastructure and setup. By product is something which is produced as a result of producing something else (the main product). Usually, the by-products are disposed of and have little value.

But in by product pricing, the by product has significant value and the manufacturer can gain competitive advantage by reducing the price of the main product or recovering some of his expenses by selling the valuable by product.

Importance of by Product Pricing

By product pricing presents an opportunity to set the right price for the by-products of the main core product so as to earn incremental revenue. It is very important to set the right price for the by-product so that it can be sold. Like any other pricing, the costs need to be properly ascertained to make sure that the by-products are still sold at profit and are able to recover costs.

Many times if done properly by maintaining quality, the by-products can become part of the portfolio and can be a strategic part of the portfolio. The pricing if done without thought can lead to unnecessary losses.

BRAND

"A brand is a name, term, design, symbol, or any other feature that identifies one seller's good or service as distinct from those of other sellers" (American Marketing Association).

Branding is the process of giving a meaning to specific organization, company, products or services by creating and shaping a brand in consumers' minds. It is a strategy designed by organizations to help people to quickly identify and experience their brand, and give them a reason to choose their products over the competition's, by clarifying what this particular brand is and is not.

Branding is important because not only is it what makes a memorable impression on consumers but it allows your customers and clients to know what to expect from your company. It is a way of distinguishing yourself from the competitors and clarifying what it is you offer that makes you the better choice. Your brand is built to be a true representation of who you are as a business, and how you wish to be perceived.

There are many areas that are used to develop a brand including advertising, customer service, social responsibility, reputation, and visuals. All of these elements (and many more) work together to create one unique and (hopefully) attention-grabbing profile.

Branding increases customers Increases business value

Improves employee pride and satisfaction Creates trust within the market place

VALUE ADDED SERVICES

"Value added services" (VASs) refer to improved or enhanced versions of standard and basic core network services provided over telecommunication networks that include voice calls and all forms of data transmission including fax, short message services SMSs and Multi-media services (MMSs) normally accessed at extra costs than the basic services.

The goal of supply chains is to add value to the manufacturing and distribution processes. Supply chains can be differentiated based on characteristics such as price, time reliability, and risk, depending on the markets and value chains they serve.

There have never been more product choices in the marketplace than there are now, thanks to globalization and technical developments in supply chain management.

Furthermore, whether purchased in a store or plucked right from their doorstep, buyers want to receive their products immediately and in excellent condition. That indicates that having popular products isn't enough to guarantee success.

Today, they must also arrive swiftly, effectively, and in perfect condition, or you risk losing customers.

According to Gartner Glossary a value-added service (VAS) is provided by a network or its resellers to generate additional revenue by providing users with additional benefits.

The sum of SMS (Short Message Service), data-over-cellular, and information-service income is used to compute total VAS income. All other VAS revenue is deemed transparent and is accounted for as part of call costs or subscription income.

Value-added services are services that go above and beyond what your 3PL company already provides. These add-on services might assist customers to tailor their unique and evolving company requirements. Despite their differences in kind, they all have the same goal: to improve efficiency, capabilities, and help businesses stay competitive in their markets.

Finding out if your provider offers these next-level services are critical because they can make a significant difference in your overall logistics process. According to Adelanto SCM's recentresearch, 63 percent of organizations that use value-added services consider it a "very significant" business function.

Examples of the value-added logistics and supply chain services are:

- Packaging
- Record Retention
- Assembly
- Consolidation
- Inspection
- Inventory Management
- Reverse Logistics
- Sorting
- Trans loading Transportation Management
- Direct Store Pickup
- Tailoring
- Labeling
- Replacement

STRATEGIC PRICING

Strategic pricing is a method of pricing a product or service based on its value to the consumer or another competitive approach. A company can choose a specific pricing strategy based on its objectives. Strategic pricing sets a product's price based on the product's value to the customer, or on competitive strategy, rather than on the cost of production.

Types of strategic pricing:

1. Market penetration pricing

Market penetration pricing is where businesses set a low initial price for goods and services. The business hopes to gain consumer attention and build a loyal customer base. Eventually, most businesses increase prices once they have a steady customer base.

If you choose to establish a market penetration pricing strategy, you will most likely be met with slim profits off the bat.

You could also experience a price war between competitors, which can be difficult for small companies. Small businesses might not have the ability to drop down to the same low prices as larger companies.

Increasing the price after the product has been on the market will probably lead to an increase in profits. But, you could lose some customers as a result of the higher prices.

Market penetration can be good for building a customer base. But, it might not be the best strategy if you need to make high profits immediately. Small businesses could have some problems using this pricing strategy.

1. Price skimming pricing

Price skimming is the opposite of market penetration pricing. With price skimming, businesses initially set high prices in the hopes of turning a quick profit. Usually, businesses lower their prices once other companies offer competitive pricing.

If you choose to use price skimming pricing, you could be met with high profits off the bat. But, you need to be aware that some consumers will be turned away by the price. Oppositely, high prices can lead customers to believe they are getting a quality good or service.

Typically, you want to use price skimming strategies when you first introduce a product to the market.

Use the price skimming strategy when you introduce a brand new product, service, or feature that not many other businesses have. Because of the lack of competition, you can get away with charging higher prices, as long as there is demand for it.

With price skimming pricing, you will experience high profit margins when you first release the good or service. Eventually, your profit margin will be slimmer once other businesses offer the same thing at competitive prices.

3. Economy pricing

Economy pricing is one strategy that prices certain products and services at a low rate. With economy pricing, businesses cut down on the costs that go into making the product or performing the services. The prices are low because the products are generic.

With economy pricing strategies in marketing, your products would attract consumers who aren't willing to pay high prices. Many grocery and retail stores, like Wal-Mart, use an economy pricing strategy for their products.

Small businesses might have more trouble using this pricing policy. Large businesses might benefit more from economy pricing because they can obtain bulk items and turn profits.

As a small business owner, you don't want to price your products or services too low. Economy pricing is a great way to attract a variety of people, but you also want to make sure you have a decent profit margin.

4. Competitive pricing

Competitive pricing is where businesses base their prices on what competitor's charge. Many businesses opt for competitive pricing to stick out from other businesses. With competitive pricing, the business hopes customers will choose the less expensive product.

If you offer competitive pricing for similar products or services, you will need to stay up- to-date on what other businesses are charging. You should do a competitive pricing analysis and study competitors.

You can offer customers a price matching offer. With a price matching offer, you vow to match a competitor's price if a customer brings it to your attention.

You might consider a competitive pricing strategy if your products or services don't vary from other businesses. However, competitive pricing can lead to narrow profit margins, so don't use this strategy for all your offerings.

5. Discount pricing

Discount pricing is a strategy where a business marks down the prices of goods or services in an effort to attract customers. Many times, the price discounts last only a short time. Sometimes, the discounts are given to products or services that were originally overpriced.

Discount pricing is also good to use toward the end of a product's life cycle. You can clear your business's inventory with discount pricing. For example, you have meat that is going to go bad in a few days. Instead of wasting it, offer it at a discounted price.

If you use the discount pricing method, you might see an increase in customers and sales. But, you want to be wary of marking down items too much. Leave yourself enough room to make a profit.

Big businesses might have more success doing discount pricing compared to smaller businesses. If you decide to use a discount pricing strategy, don't try to compete with what large businesses can do.

6. Psychological pricing

Psychological pricing is when a customer thinks they are getting a good deal. There are different types of psychological pricing:

- Charm pricing: using numbers that end in "9" (i.e., $24.99 vs. $25.00)
- Prestige pricing: using rounded numbers (i.e., $25.00 vs. $24.99)
- BOGO pricing: buy one, get one free discounts

Any business can take advantage of psychological pricing. Whenever you try to make a price look more appealing to a customer, you are using psychological pricing.

7. Bundled pricing

Lastly, bundled pricing is another strategy many businesses use. Bundled pricing is just like it sounds: businesses bundle multiple goods or services together and give consumers a lower price than if they purchased the items separately.

For example, you offer cable, WIFI, and phone services. You might set up a pricing strategy that looks like this:

- Cable: Rs 49.95

- WIFI: Rs 55.00
- Phone: Rs 24.99
- Bundled (cable, Wi-Fi, and phone): Rs 84.99

The customer saves money if they bundle all three products instead of buying them separately.

Bundling encourages customers to purchase more products or services, which means more money for your business.

Smart Pricing:

Smart pricing is a strategy where you set dynamic pricing rules based on changing market conditions. It includes monitoring competitor prices and frequently adjusting prices against competitors to offer competitive deals while protecting your profit margins.

What are the 5 pricing strategies?

The 5 most common pricing strategies

- Cost-plus pricing. Calculate your costs and add a mark-up.
- Competitive pricing. Set a price based on what the competition charges.
- Price skimming. Set a high price and lower it as the market evolves.
- Penetration pricing.
- Value-based pricing.

Pricing strategies to attract customers to your business

- Price skimming.
- Market penetration pricing.
- Premium pricing.

- Economy pricing.
- Bundle pricing.
- Value-based pricing.
- Dynamic pricing.

CUSTOMER VALUE MEASURES

Customer value measures a product or service's worth and compares it to its possible alternatives. This determines whether the customer feels like they received enough value for the price they paid for the product/service.

Customer value can encompass many factors: your brand's reliability, the effort level they need to put in to get what they want, how innovative your products are, how useful your services are, how they feel about your public image, and how successful their interactions with you are.

Measuring all these factors can seem daunting, but at the end of the day, customer value can be best measured by answering the following questions:

- What are the customer benefits?
- What are the customer costs?

Measuring customer benefits

Customer benefits can include:

- The quality of your product or service
- Your public image and <u>company values</u>
- Your ability to provide a <u>better offering than competitors</u>

- The <u>customer experience</u> you provide
- The quality of your <u>customer service</u>
- The value you impart on them when they choose to buy with you

Some of these are easier to measure than others. For example, you can survey customers with simple binary or multiple choice questions to get feedback on customer experience and product quality – but understanding the social benefit of choosing you over another brand is harder to quantify.

Continually reviewing customer feedback and collating data will help you to determine what benefits attract customers. Using scoring metrics and feedback from the customer can help to pinpoint what benefits matter most, so you can act accordingly.

Measuring customer costs

Customer costs can be divided into two types: the tangible operational data that can be proven) and the intangible (how your customer feels about your product and how much they invest in your brand).

Tangible costs might include:

- The financial cost of your product or service
- Upfront costs, such as installation or on boarding fees
- Maintenance costs
- Renewal or repurchasing costs
- Access costs for your product or service

The costs that are hard to quantify are:

- Bad customer experience
- The time it takes to make a purchase
- The emotional cost of engaging with your brand and making a purchase
- The social cost of choosing you over competitors
- The time cost of undergoing the learning curve for your products or services

The costs that are easier to quantify can easily be gauged through your operational data. For the intangible costs, gather real-time feedback from customers so you get data that's honest and relevant. Customer surveys and other feedback channels will help you to measure these more difficult metrics.

What is Customer Value?

Customer Value is the incremental benefit which a customer derives from consuming a product after paying in return. The term value signifies the benefit that a customer gets from a product. It is the difference between the benefits (sum of tangible and intangible benefits) and the cost.

Customer Value Parameters

The image below shows the different parameters which can determine the actual customer value delivered to customer from the marketer or manufacturer.

Customer value formulas

Once you've calculated the monetary and personal benefits and costs of engaging with your brand, you can then calculate your customer value.

Customer value can be calculated using a simple formula:

(Total Customer Benefits - Total Customer Costs) = Customer Value, or (B - C = CV).

The benefits for the customer must outweigh the costs to result in a higher customer value.

The calculation for customers choosing your product or service can also be captured in a formula:

$(Value^1 — Price^1) > (Value^2 — Price^2)$

$Value^1$ is the value of your product or service in your customer's eyes. $Price^1$ is the cost of that product or service. $Value^2$ and $Price^2$ are the same for the next best alternative from your competitor.

This formula simply means that the value of your product (minus the price it costs) must be more than that of the best alternative. Your customers must see your value as being worth the cost, and that your offering is worth more than the next best thing.

Obviously, these formulas won't provide you with a neat financial sum in the end. However, calculating whether your customers think the benefits are worth the cost of buying your offering – and understanding the factors that go into that decision – will help you to maintain and improve your customer value.

Reference

Books:

1. W.J. Hopp and M.L. Spearman. Factory Physics: Foundations of Manufacturing Management. Irwin, McGraw-Hill, 1996.
2. N. Viswanadham. Analysis of Manufacturing Enterprises. Kluwer Academic Publishers, 2000.
3. Sridhar Tayur, Ram Ganeshan, Michael Magazine (editors). Quantitative Models for Supply Chain Management. Kluwer Academic Publishers, 1999.
4. R.B. Handfield and E.L. Nochols, Jr. Introduction to Supply Chain Management. Prentice Hall, 1999.
5. N. Viswanadham and Y. Narahari. Performance Modeling of Automated manufacturing Systems. Prentice Hall of India, 1998.
6. Sunil Chopra and Peter Meindel. Supply Chain Management: Strategy, Planning, and Operation, Prentice Hall of India, 2002.
7. Jeremy F. Shapiro. Modeling the Supply Chain. Duxbury Thomson Learning, 2001.
8. David Simchi Levi, Philip kaminsky, and Edith Simchi Levi. Designing and Managing the Supply Chain: Concepts, Strategies, and Case Studies. Irwin McGrawHill, 2000.

Articles

1. Y. Narahari and S. Biswas. Supply Chain Management: Models and Decision Making.
2. Ram Ganeshan and Terry P. Harrison. An Introduction

to Supply Chain Management.

3. D. Connors, D. An, S. Buckley, G. Feigin, R. Jayaraman, A. Levas, N. Nayak, R. Petrakian, R. Srinivasan. Dynamic modelling for business process reengineering. IBM Research Report 19944, 1995.

4. Anthony Chavez, Pattie Maes, Kasbah: An Agent Marketplace for Buying and Selling Goods.

5. Anthony Chavez, Daniel Dreilinger, Robert Guttman, Pattie Maes, A Real-Life Experiment in Creating an Agent Marketplace.

6. Gaurav Tewari, Pattie Maes, Design and Implementation of an Agent-Based Intermediary Infrastructure for Electronic Markets.